# Candle Making Genius

## How To Make Candles That Look Beautiful & Amaze Your Friends

### By Beth Shaw

A catalogue record of this book is available at the British Library.

## Exclusive Free Offer

Join other 'Candle Makers' and owners in our unique **FREE** club – Exclusive to owners of this book.

See page 24 on how to join easily in seconds (and free).

Receive discounts on candle supplies like wicks, molds and wax. Connect with other members to share knowledge and experience, or ask questions. The best place for people who want to make wonderful candles.

# Foreword

Candles have been in use as a source of illumination for at least 5,000 years. The ancient Egyptians used a form of candles, but without a wick, an innovation credited to the Romans. (The Chinese and Japanese began using wicks in their candles at roughly the same time.)

Many cultures incorporated candles into their religious practices, and there are multiple references to candles in the Bible. By the Middle Ages in Europe, the use of candles was strictly the purview of the church and the aristocracy.

Candles in that period were made primarily of rendered animal fat until the introduction of cleaner burning beeswax. The crafting of candles was considered an art, so that candle making guilds were common in England and France in the 13th century.

These candle makers ran thriving shops, or made house calls, creating candles on site from kitchen fat saved specifically for that purpose.

When Europeans crossed the Atlantic and began to colonize the Americas, new innovations in candle making resulted.

Colonial American women boiled bayberries to create a sweet smelling wax that burned with very little smoke. These candles were superseded by those fabricated of whale oil in the 18th century.

# Foreword

Wax from whale oil created harder, more durable candles that did not soften and bend during the hot summer months.

The 19th century provided both the greatest innovations to date in the manufacture of candles, and their demise as a primary form of light.

In the 1820s, French chemist Michel Eugene Chevreul extracted stearic acid from animal fat that, when added to candles, increases their burn time and opacity.

Joseph Morgan built a machine in 1834 for the continuous creating of molded candles, making lighting affordable for the masses for the first time, a trend enhanced by the introduction of cheaper paraffin wax in the 1850s.

This golden age of candle use was, however, short lived. In 1879, Thomas Edison invented the light bulb. As electric light gained in popularity, candle use declined.

By the latter half of the 20th century, the once ubiquitous lighting was reserved primarily for decorative items and as an emergency expedient.

In the 1990s, however, the development of soybean wax marked the first real advance in candle making in more than a century.

# Foreword

This slower burning material creates fewer emissions than paraffin candles and has been embraced by 21$^{st}$ century candle makers as an environmentally friendly addition to their very old and time-honored craft.

As a mood setter or a novelty gift item, candles have not lost their powerful charm. No light is as soft and gentle as that cast by candles, and their very creation seems to take us back to a time when the pace of life was slower.

Whether you are considering making candles for fun or profit, the purpose of this book is to give you a solid foundation to understand and take up the process.

The 18$^{th}$ century scientist Georg Lichtenberg said, "Man loves company - even if it is only that of a small burning candle."

There is perhaps no more companionable craft than candle making and it's my pleasure to offer you an introduction to what I hope will be for you the good friend it has been for me.

## Table of Contents

# Table of Contents

# Table of Contents

# Table of Contents

# Table of Contents

Table of Contents

# Table of Contents

# Chapter 1 – Types of Candles

The survival of the humble candle in the age of the glaring electrical glow of the light bulb is a clear testament to the comforting and almost magical allure of a small, flickering flame.

Though tiny in their scope, candles were, for centuries, man's light in the dark of night and they remain a beloved part of cultures around the world.

## Structure of a Candle

Candles are one of those items we don't think about. We just know they work. When you really stop and think about how they work, however, candles are an amazingly innovative system of lighting comprised of two key components:

- Wax for fuel.
- A wick to create light from the fuel.

Together, these components create a highly contained system that is portable and can be manufactured from a variety of sources.

In an emergency, you can even take a wrapped stick of butter, insert a wick made of nothing more than rolled toilet paper, and it will burn.

## The Candle Wick

Wicks are highly absorbent and draw fuel into themselves by the force of capillary action. In technical terms, this is defined as:

"the ability of a liquid to flow in narrow spaces without the assistance of, and in opposition to, external forces like gravity."

Basically, the wick draws up the liquid so that a constant supply is being fed to the flame. The fire both creates the light and melts the wax to keep the supply of liquid wax constant.

# Chapter 1 – Types of Candles

## The Candle Fuel

A variety of fuels have been used in candles, with paraffin wax being one of the more dominant in modern times. As candles have evolved, there has been a continual effort to improve the quality of the self-contained fuel so that it would:

- burn longer
- provide a better quality of light
- smell good
- give off fewer emissions like sooty smoke

Although there have been material improvements in candle design over the last 5,000 years, they have continued to be used as a source of illumination. The basic elegant theory that makes the "simple" candle work has remained unaltered.

## Versatile Form Factors

Given the basic function of the candle, its practical application has taken on many forms, some largely ceremonial and others highly utilitarian.

## Tapers

Tapers are tall, thin, cylindrical candles generally created by dipping to create a very smooth, well-finished

---

appearance. They can, however, be poured into molds or even rolled.

Tapers must be placed in a candleholder for burning and are often used in elegant dinner settings and religious ceremonies.

The diameter of a taper is generally 0.5 to 0.875 in/ 1.27-2.22 cm in diameter.

Pillars

Pillar candles are created in molds and are designed to be freestanding on heat-resistant plates or pans. They are made of hard waxes that retain its shape.

Typically cylindrical in diameters of 1-4 in / 2.54-10.16 cm, pillar candles burn evenly for a long time with minimal dripping.

They are often referred to by diameter and height, so a 3 x 6 inch pillar is 3 inches wide and six inches tall (7.62 cm x 15.24 cm).

Pillars are decorative in nature, but they are also good for emergency uses like power outages.

Container, Jar, or Filled

The terms container, jar, and filled candle are all synonymous. Available in a range of receptacles from apothecary jars to tins, these candles are designed to be self-contained, with no dripping.

Container candles are made from soft waxes that would not be able to stand on their own. They are also decorative in nature, but tend to have a long burn time and are also good as emergency lighting.

## Votive

Votive candles are widely used for religious purposes. They are typically 1.5 in / 3.81 cm in diameter and 2 in / 5.08 cm tall.

These candles are often burned as an offering accompanying a prayer. They can also be used as small decorative candles, and are typically rated for 10-15 hour burn times.

## Gel Candle

Gel candles are made from mineral-based products and have unfairly been deemed dangerous due to a flooding of the market with poorly made decorative candles.

Candles made from gel can only be used in containers. The material lacks the rigidity to be formed into pillars. Additionally, the thicker the gel, the hotter it will become over time, thus limiting the potential physical size of the finished product.

Nothing should be embedded in the gel that can, with an increase in heat, catch fire.

## Tea Light

Tea lights are small, circular candles encased in metal cups. They are often used as warmers for items like teapots, fondue pots, potpourri warms, casserole warmers, and similar items. Their burn time is approximately 3-5 hours.

## Luminaria

A luminaria is not a candle per se, but a type of "lantern" made from a small paper bag weighted down with sand. A small candle, generally a votive or a tea candle is placed inside.

Luminarias are popular during the Christmas holiday season, particularly in the American Southwest, to create an outdoor lighting display.

## Methods for Making Candles

Although not all of these methods continue to be widely practiced today, there are many ways to create useful and beautiful candles.

Some candle makers actually enjoy fabricating their candles from older and more traditional methods not only for the finished product, but for the experience of doing something "the old-fashioned way."

### Molded

Molded candles are frequently referred to as "cast" candles. Hot wax is poured into a pre-formed mold to create this type of candle.

A mold can be almost anything that will withstand the heat of the wax and allow the candle to be removed when cool. Commercial molds are typically made of metal.

### Dipped

As the name implies, dipped candles are created by repeatedly dipping a wick into a container of melted wax. When the desired density is achieved, the candle is complete.

Typically tapers are made by dipping, a process that allows the long, elegant candles to achieve their distinctive, smooth lines.

## Drawn

Drawn candles are made by a much older method that can create a highly unique candle capable of burning a very long time.

A long length of wick, usually several yards, is pulled through melted wax and often wound into coils held in special burners. This type of candle does not require a dense amount of wax to have a reliable source of fuel.

# Chapter 1 – Types of Candles

Drawn candles of the coiled variety are not only useful for their long life, but also for their compact form factor. They have become popular again in recent years as novelty and nostalgic items.

## Machine Made Candles

One machine method for manufacturing candles allows for wax to be extruded through a shaped template. The candles are then cut into appropriate lengths.

Pressed candles are formed from beads of atomized wax in a cooling drum that are compressed into molds during the manufacturing process.

The force of the compression binds the wax, allowing the finished candle to be removed quickly from the mold without a prolonged period of cooling.

## Candles and Fire Safety

In the United States alone, on an annual basis, more than 15,000 house fires are attributed to the unsafe burning of candles. Regardless of the form factor of candle involved, the following safety precautions are necessary for their safe use.

### Burn in Plain Sight

Keep a burning candle in plain sight. Do not leave a candle burning unattended in any room in the house, and put out all candles before going to sleep at night. This means that the wick should no longer be smoking and no glowing ember should be present. Do not use a candle as a night light.

## Observe What's Close By

Pay careful attention to the area adjacent to the burning candle. Do not light candles near flammable items like curtains or drapery, bedding, carpet or rugs, books and paper, or any flammable decorations.

## Out of Reach of Children and Pets

Place all burning candles safely out of the reach of children and pets. Burning candles are easily knocked over by rambunctious horseplay and can ignite household furnishings much more rapidly than you realize.

## Trim the Wick

Before lighting a candle, trim the wick down to 0.25 inch /0.64 cm to avoid uneven burning and dripping of hot wax.

## Use Real Candle Holders

Use only holders that are designed for use with a candle to ensure that the item is appropriately sturdy, heat resistant, and large enough to contain a volume of melted wax.

**Level, Heat Resistant Surfaces**

Place all burning candles, in and out of holders, on heat resistant, level, stable surfaces. Failure to do so can cause the underlying surface to heat up and ignite, or to be damaged from the heat of the burning candle.

**Avoid Accumulated Debris**

Do not allow debris to accumulate in the wax pool including dropped matches.

**Read Safety Instructions**

If the candle is made of a special material, like gel, and comes with safety instructions, read the enclosure and follow the recommendations to the letter.

**Avoid Drafts and Air Currents**

Avoid placing candles in areas that are subject to draft from windows, ceiling fans, and other sources. The movement of the air can lead to rapid and uneven burning that can cause flare-ups of the flame and create soot.

Additionally, lightweight objects may be blown into the candle flame and catch fire. Do burn candles in rooms that are well ventilated.

## Don't Let Candles Burn All the Way Down

Extinguish a candle's flame as it reaches the bottom of the container. Typically, you should stop burning a candle when 2 in / 5.08 cm of wax remains in a free-standing candle or there is only 0.5 inch / 1.27 cm of wax left in a container.

## Be Aware of Hot Wax

Do not touch the hot wax pool in any burning candle, and place burning candles at a distance of at least 3 in / 7.62 cm apart to avoid the candles melting into one another.

## Use a Candle Snuffer

When extinguishing a candle, use a candle snuffer. Do not put a candle out with water, as this will cause the hot wax to splutter and may cause a hot glass container to shatter.

## Don't Walk with a Lit Candle

When using candles during a power outage, make sure they are placed on a level, safe space well away from any flammable items. Do not move around the house with a lit candle.

**Extinguish Malfunctioning Candles**

Immediately extinguish any candle that smokes, flickers constantly, or that develops a high flame. The candle is not functioning as it should, and is therefore unsafe. Trim the wick, allow the candle to cool, and make sure there is no draft in the area before lighting the candle again.

# Exclusive FREE Offer – How to Join

Join other 'Candle Makers' in our unique **FREE** club – Exclusive to owners of this book.

It's quick and easy to sign up. You can receive discounts on wax, wicks, molds and more including connecting with other candle makers. Here's how in 2 simple steps…

**Step 1**

Go to http://www.CandleMakingGenius.com
Enter your name and email address and click 'Join.'

**Step 2**

Confirm your subscription. As soon as you sign up we'll send you an email asking you to confirm the details are correct. Just click the link in the email and you'll be joined free.

If you don't receive the email please check your spam folder and that you used the correct email address.

It's as easy as that. Any questions please email support@candlemakinggenius.com  and where possible we will help.

## Chapter 2 – Making Candles

The only way to really get a feel for the experience of making candles is to make candles! The following material will take you from working with a starter "kit" through purchasing basic equipment.

I'll also describe various types of candle making processes to give you a feel for the direction you want to take in the beginning.

If you're a "crafty" sort you'll know what I mean when I say, start slow! Anyone who has ever fallen for the lure of beautiful yarn or gorgeous paints will immediately understand what I'm talking about.

You may well wind up with blocks and blocks of wax and a huge assortment of dyes and scents before all is said and done, but make sure you really want to become a candle maker before making that investment!

## Starter Kits for Candle Making

As a novice candle maker, I recommend that you purchase a candle making kit to see if this is truly a hobby (or vocation) you will enjoy.

To get a reasonably complete introduction to the process, any kit you purchase should be sufficiently all-inclusive to familiarize you with the major steps of the process and potentially give you a jump-start on your store of equipment and supplies.

Start with a container candle kit. Most of these products will allow you to make 8-12 candles. The containers (jars or tins) should be included.

Even if you decide candle making isn't for you, exploring via this route will leave you with candles to burn in your own home, or to give away as gifts — probably with a good story about your "adventure" in creating them.

The kit you purchase will likely contain at least 10 lbs / 4.5 kg of wax and should also come with a pouring pot, a thermometer, pre-tabbed wicks, and an assortment of fragrance oils and dye chips as well as complete instructions.

The included components will vary by kit, but don't settle for less than these minimum requirements or you won't get a good introduction to the process.

(Refer to the back of this book for online candle supply companies. Many of them offer very good, complete introductory candle kits.)

To buy a candle making kit with this amount of materials you will pay approximately $75 / £46.

Since you will need a heat source, most people make their first batch of candles in the kitchen. Before you start your project, take precautions to cover and protect your countertops. Candle dye will stain.

If you stick with candle making, you may well want to relocate to the garage or to a craft or utility room and switch to a hot plate or portable burner.

The bigger your candle projects, the more you will want to be able to spread out to work. Like any craft, candle makers accumulate equipment, and it's good to have a dedicated workspace.

If you do opt to use a hot plate, make sure the unit is well away from any potentially flammable materials. Always turn off and unplug the burner when you leave the room.

Set aside a whole afternoon to make your candles on a day when you won't be interrupted. Your first batch will go very slowly because you'll be concentrating on doing everything right.

Future projects will go much more quickly, and you'll be surprised how many candles you'll be able to produce as you become more proficient.

## Okay, I'm Hooked

If you make a set of candles with your first kit, and you're hooked, immediately start investing in your own equipment and supplies rather than continuing with more kits.

These sets are a fantastic way to get started, but they're expensive and repetitive if you use them over and over. Next thing you know, you'll have a dozen pouring pots on your shelf!

## Think About Your Work Space

To really set up shop, find some dedicated work and storage space. As you acquire more supplies, you'll want to be able to organize them and to find what you need easily and quickly.

There's nothing to say that you can't continue to use your kitchen and stove, but that can get problematic if you have wax melting in the pot and your family would much rather you were getting supper ready.

Additionally, it's to your advantage to work uninterrupted. Although you don't have to be a chemist to make candles, taking weights and measurements is part of the process. Getting distracted can mean a ruined batch of candles.

Deciding on your workspace first will help you to make reasonable choices about picking both your supplies and your implements, and to make any necessary modification to the area.

Since you'll probably wind up working with some type of portable burner, you may need to incorporate fire safety precautions including installing a smoke alarm and buying a fire extinguisher.

All of these considerations are highly individual choices that are dependent entirely on the configuration of your home. Try to make at least some of these decisions in advance, however, before you're staring at a mountain of candle making supplies with no idea where to put them, much less use them.

## Buying Basic Equipment

Some of the items you will purchase will be specific to the types of candles you choose to make. However, the basics to get started will include:

- wax or waxes depending on type
- fragrance oils
- dyes (sold as chips, blocks, or liquids)
- wicks and wick tabs
- a wick setting tool and/or wick bars
- a scale (preferably digital)
- a heat source
- a pouring pot(s)*
- thermometer (capable of reading up to 300 °F / 149 °C)

* As you become more advanced as a candle maker, you may have a labeled pouring pot per fragrance you use. This will prevent any unwanted — and unpleasant — scent combinations.

You'll also want a calculator, notebook, paper towels, rubbing alcohol, disposable latex gloves, scissors, and a good supply of newspapers for your work surface. Although we're talking about container candles at the moment, when you progress to molded candles, invest in a can of aerosol mold release spray.

(For the first molded project you can get away with using non-stick cooking spray.)

Mold release spray sells for approximately $12 / £7 a can.

For a more accurate buying guide for equipment and supplies, pick a set of step-by-step instructions for the candles you want to make, and purchase all of the necessary items in advance, including containers.

Handle the equipment in advance so you know how to use everything, including how to read the thermometer and scale.

Note that most digital scales will require calibration before being put to practical use.

(See Appendix 1 at the back of this book for online sources to purchase candle making supplies.)

## Acquiring More Equipment

As you move on to more advanced candle projects, these are some of the additional items you will want to have on hand:

- A ladle to transfer melted wax from one location to another when pouring is not the optimum solution.

- A metal can at least 12 in / 30.48 cm deep for making tapers.

- A sharp utility knife, a metal straight edge, and a large cutting board for cutting sheets of wax. Keep a hammer on hand to break up wax blocks into smaller pieces.

- Additional pouring pots preferably spouted. (Label these if you prefer to use a single pot for specific wax color and scent combinations.)

- Weights used to keep filled molds secured in water. (You can use almost anything for a weight, from a brick to scrap metal, but keep a variety of sizes on hand.

- Wooden dowels to make relief holes in wax and to center wicks. (This is an older method than using a metal wick bar, but it is still effective.)

- Mold sealant or masking tape to cover the holes in the bottom of molds to prevent wax leaks when pouring.

- Mold release spray.

- A set of pliers for pulling wicks through molds.

This is not an all-inclusive list. Everyone's workspace is different and crafters of all types have their favorite tools, some purchased and others creatively engineered out of their own imagination to address a specific problem.

Be open to letting your workroom evolve as it will, and don't be afraid to think outside of the box.

### Equipment for Dipped Candles

The technique for making dipped candles is relatively simple – immersing a wick in hot wax over and over to achieve a desired diameter.

This highly traditional, hands on method can be achieved through a variety of methods. The most common approach is to dip candles in pairs.

A length of wick is cut long enough to make two candles. Weights are applied to each end to keep the wicks straight. The entire piece is draped over a spacer or frame to keep the two candles separated. The "spacer" can be something as simple as a large wooden dowel, or a square of plywood or heavy cardboard with notches to secure the wicks in place.

To dip candles, you will need a dipping can that is at least 2 in / 5.08 cm longer than the finished candle. Washers, nuts, or even small fighting weights can be used to anchor each end of the wick.

The process will also call for a bucket, tall enough for the candles to be submerged in water, and hooks or pegs on which the finished candles can be hanged for drying.

Stay Safe!

In addition to maintaining a functioning smoke detector in your candle making room, also have a fire extinguisher on hand.

If you do have to put out a fire, stay calm. First, turn off any source of heat, and then use the most appropriate and expedient means to put out the flames.

- A fire extinguisher. Chose an ABC model that is rated to put out ordinary household fires that start with common combustibles, flammable liquids, and electrical fires.

- A metal pan lid. Remember that when a fire is starved of oxygen, it goes out.
- Common household baking soda. This is a tried and true means of smothering flames.

Damp towels will also work to deprive a fire of oxygen and help to extinguish the flames.

DO NOT under any circumstances ever try to put out a wax fire with water. The wax will splatter. This can spread the fire, and the hot wax may seriously burn you.

## Types of Wax

As the primary "fuel" of your candle, the type of wax you choose is arguably the most important decision in any project you undertake.

Most modern candles are made of either paraffin or beeswax, although soy and gel candles have become popular in recent years.

Although wax types melt uniformly, the products are typically sold as:

- blocks
- flakes
- sheets

The different forms can be more applicable by the type of candle you're making. Sheets of wax, for instance, are required to make rolled candles, a process described in the "How To" section of this book.

Beeswax

Bees secrete beeswax as they build the combs in which they store honey and incubate larvae. When the honey is removed from the hives by beekeepers, they melt down the honeycomb and sell it in blocks.

The sweet-smelling wax is a golden yellow brown unless it has been filtered or bleached to a pure white. In candles, beeswax burns slowly and creates a gentle, glowing light.

When beeswax is blended with paraffin, the resulting candles are both affordable and long lasting.

A one-pound block (0.45 kg) of organic beeswax retails for approximately $10 / £6.17.

Paraffin

Paraffin candle waxes are made from the by-products of petroleum products. They have variable melting points rated low, medium, and high.

# Chapter 2 – Making Candles

For the purpose of making candles, the melting point should fall in a range of 125-150 °F / 51.7-65.6 °C.

Generally, stearic acid is added to paraffin to make the resulting candles harder and more opaque, which improves their light.

For candle making purposes, paraffin is generally sold in "blends" by candle type, for instance "container blend" or "pillar" blend.

There may also be a descriptive added to these products for the finished level of opacity, for instance "creamy" or "translucent." While these things refer to the properties of the wax, they do not affect price significantly.

A 10 lbs (4.53 kg) lot of paraffin sells for approximately $15 / £9.26, with a 60 lbs / 27.21 kg carton selling for $135 / £83.40.

## Candle Gel

Candle gel has been used in candle making since the 1990s. It is not wax, but rather a mineral oil combined with a gelatinizing polymer.

The resulting substance feels rubbery, and stays solid at room temperature.

The product is sold as Versagel C, and is trademarked by Penreco. It comes in three grades:

- Versagel C LP, suitable for clear candles
- Versagel C MP, for medium to high fragrance loads
- Versagel C HP, for high fragrances and the suspension of pigments and decorative particles

According to claims made by the manufacturer, candles made from Versagel will burn 5 times longer than traditional forms of wax.

Because the product cannot be formed with sufficient rigidity to stand alone, gels are used in container candles only.
There have been concerns expressed about emissions from these candles, although Penreco maintains the gel has been proven to be safe in extensive testing.

It is important to note that gel candles do burn very hot. This creates a real danger of spontaneous combustion if flammable decorative materials are suspended in the substance.

Although prices vary by sources, Versagel sells for approximately $25 / £15.44 per 5 lbs / 2.27 kg.

Soy Wax

Soy is a modern, ecologically friendly vegetable wax that creates fewer emissions. It burns slower than traditional waxes, thus extending the life of the candle.

Soy wax is sold both as a pure wax and blended with paraffin. While soy waxes are more expensive, both in raw and finished candles, they do burn longer and cleaner.

Soy wax sells for approximately $18 / £11.12 per 6 lbs / 2.72 kg, or $97 / £60 per 50 lbs / 22.68 kg.

Doing Your Wax "Math"

Most beginners are drawn up short by the question, "How much wax do I need?"

The answer is another question, "What kind of wax are you using?" All types of solid wax yield different amounts of melted wax.

Any calculations for wax usage depend on how much liquid melted wax each type will produce. Start with these figures to make your calculations:

- 1 lbs / 0.45 kg paraffin = 20 oz / 567 g melted liquid

- 1 lbs / 0.45 kg soy wax = 18 oz / 510 g melted liquid

- 1 lbs / 0.45 kg beeswax = 16 oz / 454 g melted liquid

Let's look at an example for calculating the amount of wax needed for container candles.

1. Using your scale, weigh one of your containers and write down the amount.

2. Fill the container with water and weigh it again. Write down that amount.

3. Subtract the empty weight from the filled weight.

For the purposes of our example, let's say you have an 8 oz / 227 g container. You want to make 10 candles from paraffin wax.

You know that 1 lb / 0.45 kg of paraffin wax will yield 20 oz / 567 g of melted liquid.
8 ounces x 10 candles = 80 oz / 2268 g
80 ounces / 20 ounces = 4 lbs / 1.8 kg of paraffin

Over time, as you become conversant with the melted liquid yield of the waxes with which you work, these calculations will become second nature to you.

# Chapter 2 – Making Candles

## Amounts Vary by Candle Type

Obviously, the amount of wax you will need varies by the type of candle you are producing and by the method of production. The example above works for both container and molded candles.

If you plan on making dipped candles, you should start with approximately 6 lbs / 2.7 kg of wax. This amount will be sufficient to make six tapers that are roughly 10 in / 25.4 cm in length with a diameter of 0.875 in / 2.22 cm.

## Keeping a Notebook of Recipes

Like many crafts that involve weighing and measuring, candle making is not a precise science. "Recipes" are affected by a number of variables like the melting point of the chosen wax, the type of wick selected, and any additives used.

I highly recommend that you keep a notebook of your candle making recipes, taking down the names of products and any variation in workable temperatures, measurements and amounts.

My friends tease me that my candle notebook looks like a witch's book of spells. Since I think there's magic in a good candle recipe, I have to agree!

You will always want to test burn your candles, at which point inaccuracies and other problems will surface. Keep careful notes of how you correct these issues in the next batch.

Keeping a notebook will take a lot of the guesswork out of candle making and it will help you to use your supplies more efficiently. It's also a good way to keep track of products you do and don't want to use again.

As you continue to read and study the craft of candle making, you'll run into recipes online and in books. Your personal notebook is also a good place to "corral" things you want to try and to make annotations about modifications to borrowed recipes. In the end, most candle makers wind up practicing their own kind of alchemy.

One of the charming things about making candles is that you can give two candle makers the same recipe and their individual candles will still come out just a little different.

This truly is a hands on craft, and one into which you will inject your own personality, tastes, and talents. Your recipes will be your own, refined by trial and error to your way of working.

Let me share some recipe-related wisdom I've learned the hard way. Products don't always remain consistent in their manufacturing standards.

If you try the same recipe you've always used and something goes wrong, don't rule out the possibility that something has changed in your basic ingredients.

This is particularly true of dye colors and fragrance oils, which can vary widely from lot to lot. It's very common over time to have to rework the amounts of both that you use in your recipes to get the desired results.

Measurement Conversions

Don't be surprised if you find yourself forced to make measurement conversions to sort out a recipe taken from an online or book source.

Some of the thornier of these involve translating weights into volume. For instance:

- 1 lb of wax (454 g) = 1.5-2 cups or 12-16 fluid ounces

- 1 gallon of wax is 4 quarts or 3785 ml ml, which equals 6-11 lbs or 2.7-5.0 kg.

- 1 cubic foot of wax is 7.5 gallons.

These calculations can get really convoluted, especially if you were as math challenged in high school as I was! If you have a smart phone or a tablet, get a simple conversion application. It will save you hours of time and major headaches!

If you don't have a phone or tablet, just go into your computer browser and search for phrases like "convert weight to volume." You'll find links to online conversion calculators. Don't forget to bookmark them!

Any time you work out a conversion, write it all down! Personally, I've found that making candles is actually pretty easy and lots of fun, but I don't like math any better now than I did when I was in grade school.

It's not worth it to me, however, to waste time and supplies and get a bad batch of candles, so I always take the time to "do" the numbers.

## Understanding Wax Melting

You will never melt your wax directly over your heat source, instead you will use a double boiler arrangement to ensure even heating.

To achieve this arrangement, you will need a saucepan large enough to hold your pouring pot.

Position a metal trivet or something similar in the saucepan and add approximately one inch / 2.54 cm of water.

The pouring pot will sit on top of the trivet, away from the direct heat source.

Set your heat source to medium and allow the water to come to a boil. Do not, however, create a rolling boil as this will just create a mess as the water splatters out.

Use your thermometer to monitor the temperature of the wax until it reaches the desired level.

## Working with Additives

Additives can modify the performance of wax in a number of ways, changing its outward appearance or altering the burning properties and melting point.

It is rare for anything added to wax to exceed 2 percent of the total volume of the material.

### Stearic Acid

Stearic acid is a refined animal or vegetable fat sold as either a flake or powder. It is commonly added to paraffin, but not to beeswax.

Because of its caustic properties, stearic acid should never be used with rubber candle molds. Additionally, it will oxidize copper on contact.

When mixed with paraffin, stearic acid reduces the melting point and makes the candles harder and thus less susceptible to slumping or bending. Additionally, stearic acid will make the candle less transparent.

### Vybar

Vybar is a more modern alternative to stearic acid. It provides all the benefits imparted by stearic acid, but also helps to eliminate bubbles in the wax and to increase the material's ability to bind with scented oils.

There are two varieties with different melting points:

- Vybar 103, melting point 160 °F / 71.1 °C
- Vybar 260, melting point 130 °F / 54.4 °C

The recommended use is to select the Vybar that is closest to the melting point of the wax and to incorporate it at a rate of 1% by weight.

## Fisher-Tropsch Wax (FT)

The addition of Fisher-Tropsch Wax (FT), a synthetic paraffin with a high melting point of 215 °F / 101.7 °C, to candles hardens their structure and gives the wax a more translucent look.

FT is often added when the desire is to create a candle that will emit a pronounced glow through the wax.

Synthetic waxes work well in pillar candles into which surface decorations have been suspended because they will appear to be backlighted.

## Understanding Wicks

Candle makers can argue endlessly about their favored choice in almost any material they use, including wicks. This is actually understandable since there are so many types on the market, with new variations still being produced.

The longer you make candles, the more you will develop your own preferences, both for wick type and brand.

In the beginning, you may want to simply follow the recommendation for wick type listed on the packaging of the wax you purchase. These guidelines may also include suggestions for wicks by candle type and size.

Typically, wick manufacturers classify candles according to diameter:

- Extra Small, 0-1 in (0-2.54 cm)
- Small, 1-2 in (2.54 - 5.08 cm)
- Medium, 2-3 in (5.08 - 7.62 cm)
- Large, 3-4 in (7.62 - 10.16 cm)
- Extra Large, 4+ in (10.16+ cm)

Certain wicks will perform better according to candle size, wax type, and even candle shape. With experience, you will get a feel for what works best in your own projects.

The following are some of the most readily available types of wicks you will find listed in candle supply catalogs and online.

Beyond safety considerations, or carefully deciding when to use hot burning wicks like those that are paper cored and create large melt pools, there isn't necessarily a "right" answer on wick choice.

## Flat Braid

A flat braid wick is comprised of multiple braided strands rated by the number of plies used. The larger the ply number, the larger or thicker the wick.
- Extra Small, 15 ply
- Small, 18 ply
- Medium, 24-30 ply
- Large, 42 ply
- Extra Large, 60 ply

Flat braid wicks are tensioned, and have a tendency to bend over when burned. They may also burn slightly off center, leading to an uneven melt pool.

This can create a lot of messy drips if the pool reaches the edge of a pillar candle.

## Square Braid

A square braid wick looks like a series of squares with round corners. This type of wick is also rated from extra small to large, but systems to delineate the designations vary by manufacturer.

Square braid wicks stand straighter than flat braid wicks while burning. This is a desirable trait in a wick since it gives better light and decreases the chance of debris in the melt pool.

Wicks that are square braids also tend to keep the flame more accurately centered in the burn pool. Precise placement achieves a more efficient and even burn.

## Cored Wick

As the name implies, a cored wick has a central material that aids in keeping the wick upright. These materials are typically:

- paper

- cotton

- zinc

- lead

Wicks with metal cores burn hotter and are recommended for use in container candles.

Concerns over the danger of lead wicks have caused them to fall out of use. The most popular cored wicks today are made of either zinc or cotton.

Zinc cored wicks have the added advantage of remaining straighter while the candle is being poured. They have a wide application of ranges for all forms of poured candles.

## New Wick Types

In the last ten years alternative wicks have been developed that will also remain rigid, but burn hot.

These include hemp cored wicks as well as improvements to traditional braided wicks that are formed so tightly they behave as if they were made with an inner core.

Manufacturers continue to tinker with improving wick construction. Any time you decide to try a new wick, I recommend buying the least amount of the material possible.

Test the wick per candle type. Conduct a full test burn. Make notes about the wick's performance in relation to wax and candle type. Also take into consideration all additives in the mixture.

The only accurate way to know how all the components of a candle will perform together is to burn the candle.

## Wooden Wicks

Wooden wicks look rather like old-fashioned tongue depressor sticks from the doctor's office. They are cut to length and are sold with crimped tabs already in place. They come in both soft and hard wood types. Of the two, the soft wooden wicks are the most popular.

Soft wicks are actually made of two pieces of wood, although this may not be obvious when you examine the wick because the two pieces are pressed together in the manufacturing process.

The softer, wider piece of the wick produces the flame while the narrower, hard piece or "booster" is the heat source. Each piece is pre-treated for ease of ignition and more stable burning.

One charming aspect of using these wicks is that they crackle when lit, creating the illusion of time spent by the fireplace.

Be careful, however, not to use too much fragrance oil with a wooden wicked candle, or this effect will be greatly diminished.

Wooden wicks are appropriate for use in container candles only, and work equally well with either paraffin or soy wax. Large or extra-large wooden wicks should be used with soy wax, however, to ensure a good melt pool.

A wooden wick has the advantage of being rigid enough to stand upright in a container without being glued at the bottom, but it will shift when the wax is poured.

Adjusting the wick to make sure it is centered and aligned is important to achieve an efficient burn with a proper melt pool.

## Wick Techniques

The following techniques are the primary methods used to ensure correct placement and burn.

Note, however, that newer wick types like wooden wicks may require different handling. Also, it is now very simple to get pre-tabbed wicks, which cuts out one small tedious chore for you.

## Priming

All wicks must be primed or saturated with wax to take out
any trapped air. Sometimes priming simply happens as
part of the overall candle making process.

In other instances, particularly with molded candles, the
wick may need to be primed in 160 °F / 71 °C wax as a
separate process.

This simply involves dipping the wick in the wax until air
bubbles begin to exit the wick, which is then taken out of
the wax and pulled taut until it's cool and stiff.

## Tabbing

A tab is a soft metal square with a center opening into
which a wick is placed in preparation for use in a candle.

The tab serves as an anchor point at the bottom of the
candle. Pliers are used to crimp or squeeze the metal edges
of the hole around the wick to secure it in place.

## Placing a Wick

There are several different ways to place a wick in a candle.
For a poured candle, apply a dot of hot glue at the bottom
of the container. Secure the wick tab on the glue.

Loop the other end of the wick around a small wooden dowel, maintaining tension. Make sure the wick remains centered in the space.

Once the wax is poured, small adjustments can be made to make sure the wick remains properly positioned while the candle dries.

Metal wick bars are a modernization of this concept. The bar includes a slot into which the wick is drawn and held firmly. These devices come in a variety of widths and are generally more stable than dowels.

Neither of these methods is expensive. Both dowels and wick bars cost less than $1 / £0.61 each.

With dipped candles, positioning the wick is not difficult as the wick is cut to the desired length and repeatedly lowered in the wax until the candle has reached the intended diameter.

The primary challenge with dipped candles is to keep the wick straight. Depending on the method used, this may be done with hand adjustments between dips, or by using a weight on one end of the wick to maintain tension. When the candle is cooled, the weights are then cut out of the base.

Chapter 2 – Making Candles

## Measuring Fragrance Oils

One compelling reason to use only scents that have been specifically formulated for candle making is the great challenge of adding a fragrance that will actually last for the life of the candle.

It's a common complaint – and a major hurdle to overcome in candle making – that scented candles smell wonderful the first time they are burned, and never smell that good again.

When adding fragrance oils, you want your wax to have reached a temperature of 170-180 °F / 76.7-82.2 °C in the pouring pot.

The typical measurement of fragrance is 1 ounce per 1 pound of wax (28 g per 0.45 kg).

Fragrances are most accurately measured by weight, so use your scale. Often for measuring oils, it's better to use a small digital scale as they are more sensitive to lower weight amounts.

As a rule of thumb, candle wax cannot hold more than 2-3% of its total volume in scent. If you go above that ratio, the scent will ooze out of the surface of the candle as an oily film.

Using too much scent in your recipe can also cause a candle to smoke excessively, and to produce oily soot.

Like heavy perfumes, an overly scented candle creates a cloying, unpleasant smell in a room. The loveliest candles are those that add just a suggestion of a fragrance to a room as a subtle addition to the beauty of the burning flame.

## Using Essential Oils

The challenge in using essential oils in candles is the fact that they dissipate quickly in the heat of the flame. One solution is to soak the wick in essential oils before it is inserted into the candle.

As an alternative option, a few drops of scented oils can be added to the candle's melt pool. There is, however, no guarantee that the flame will pick up and carry the scent. You will have to experiment with different oils for this application to find out what works.

Don't make the mistake of putting drops of essential oil on a cold candle. The oil will evaporate quickly with the scent disappearing long before the wax even begins to melt.

Also, using oils in this way on the candle's surface will likely cause the flame to smoke heavily.

## Fragrance First, Then Color

Always add your fragrance oil first, then the desired amount of color. Remember that you cannot take color out once it's added, so go slow!

The majority of colorants used for candles are aniline dyes soluble in both waxes and oils. These products come packaged as color blocks, disks, chips, and liquids.

Prices may vary by color, but most liquid candle dyes are priced at $3-$5 / £2-£3 per half ounce / 14.17 grams.

With liquid dyes add a few drops at a time to the wax, testing the color on a small square of white paper towel.

Remember that liquid wax is always darker than cooled wax. To more accurately judge the color of the finished candle, let the test patch harden.

If you are using dye blocks, cut the block into small pieces, incorporating them slowly into the wax mixture. Again, test periodically until you get the color you want.

Dye blocks / disks sell for approximately $1 / £0.61 each.

Color flakes are a variation on solid dye packaging that offer a less expensive, bulk purchase option. Prices are typically $6-$7 / £4-£5 an ounce / 28 grams.

## Mixing Colors

Many candle makers steep natural substances like beets or herbs to create dyes for their candles. This will work, but the resulting colors will be light pastels, not the vibrant hues you can achieve with synthetic dyes.

As you become comfortable with the dying process, you can also begin to blend primary colors to achieve a broader range of hues.

You will want to make careful note of any special color formulas you develop, including the specific dye brands you used.

Dye lots are rarely consistent from one batch to the next even from a trusted manufacturer, so be prepared for the fact that when you run out of a particular set of products, your formula may no longer achieve the desired results.

As you start to play with colors, just use the basic blends we all learned in grade school:

- red + yellow = orange
- yellow + blue = green
- blue + red = purple
- red + green = brown
- green + blue = teal or turquoise

By varying the amount of each color you add to the blend, you can create literally thousands of subtle shades.

What Not to Use

Food coloring will not work as candle dye because it is a water-based product that will not mix with wax.

Crayons are made of dyed paraffin wax, but they contain other additives that will make a candle's wick sputter. The same is true of oil paint and lipstick.

In an emergency, however, and provided you have a stable place to secure the crayon upright, you can light a crayon and get 15-30 minutes of burn time.

## Adding UV Stabilizer

Candles will fade if they are exposed to either fluorescent lighting or UV light for extended periods of time. This is why candles should, if possible, be stored in a dark place.

Never place candles on display in direct sunlight. You will not only see fading, but probably distortion as the wax heats up and bends.

Some colors are more susceptible to fading over time, particularly shades of pink and purple.

A UV stabilizer is a chemical added to candle wax for the purpose of preserving the candle's true color over its lifetime.

Note that a UV stabilizer will not completely stop fading, but it will slow down the process considerably.

The standard measurement to add a UV inhibitor is 1/2 teaspoon / 2.5 g per 1 lb / 0.45 kg of wax.

## Types of Candle Molds

Although I am recommending that you begin your new craft by making container candles, I have no doubt that you will begin to branch out rapidly.

The next logical progression is to explore molded candles. They are also poured candles, but the procedures for wicking are slightly more complicated, and you will also have to free your finished candle from the form.

In the simplest terms, a mold is any container that holds poured wax while it cools into a finished candle. From there, the choice of sizes and shapes is wide open.

Molds vary in type by both structure and material. The major structural types are:

- disposable, torn or cut away
- one piece, slide off the candle
- multi-part, with seams or parting lines

Multi-part molds allow for more complex shapes. Typically in design they are created to hide the seam lines as much as possible on the finished product.

As you explore in stores and online, you will find the following types of candle molds.

Plastic

Plastic candle molds are the least expensive molds on the market, but they aren't the best. Plastic has a short working life in the world of candle making.

If you're planning on making a lot of candles, you'll want to invest in more durable molds you can reliably use over and over again.

The heat of the wax will cause plastic molds to become very brittle. However, plastic molds are easy to clean, requiring little more than soap and warm water.

Due to their low cost and low maintenance, these molds are considered a good choice for novice candle makers.

As an example of prices for plastic molds, a square 3 x 3 in / 7.62 x 7.62 cm polycarbonate mold sells for approximately $10 / £6.

Aluminum or Tin

Aluminum and tin molds are my favorites because they are heat resistant and therefore very durable. The resulting surface of the candle is smooth, without seams.

Using an aluminum or tin mold gives your candles a very professional finish. They make you look like an old pro even as a beginner and are especially good for pillars and votives.

To clean aluminum or tin molds, you simply put them in a 150 °F oven on a cookie sheet. The excess wax melts and runs down on to the sheet.

The price of these molds depends entirely on size and shape. Here are a few examples:

- A square aluminum pillar mold, 2.25 x 4.5 in / 5.72 x 11.43 cm, $7 / £4

- A round aluminum pillar mold, 3 x 9.5 in / 7.62 x 24.13 cm, $10 / £6

- A box of 12 votive candle molds, 1.75 in / 4.45 cm top diameter and 2 in / 5.08 cm high, $7 / £4.

You will also find aluminum and tin molds in unique shapes like stars, triangles, and even snowflakes.

Rubber

These highly flexible molds are actually made of silicone, polyurethane, or latex. The major downside to using these products is that they can have a strong smell that is transferred to your finished candle.

Flexible molds do carry the advantage of easy release. You can get a candle out of these molds without a release spray and with very little effort on your part.

As an example of the cost of these molds, a large 5 x 4 in / 12.7 x 10.16 cm oval rubber mold retails for approximately $35 / £22.

Do-It-Yourself Molds

The use of latex as a candle mold does raise the prospect of creating completely unique do-it-yourself forms for your candles.

By applying multiple coats of liquid latex to common household items, or "finds" in architectural and salvage stores, you can create stunning, one-of-a-kind candles.

This is, however, a time-consuming project. You will need to apply approximately 10 coats of latex to the item you're molding. Allow for one hour of drying time for each layer.

The latex is applied with a paintbrush. Do not apply the material to unvarnished painted items or the paint will come off when the finished mold is removed.

Because liquid latex contains 40-50% ammonia per volume, be sure to work in a well-ventilated area. Shake the bottle of liquid latex before you begin to apply the material, and continue to shake it periodically as you work.

Shaking the latex keeps the liquid good and thick, but don't overdo it or you'll get bubbles built up in the material.

Place the object to be coated on wax paper. Try to apply each coat as evenly as possible, paying close attention to hard-to-reach spots to ensure you are getting a complete application.

After the last layer is completely dry, remove the wax paper carefully so as not to leave any fragments behind. Coat your fingers with a small amount of dishwashing liquid and use it to cover the surface of the mold.

The application of the dish soap prevents the mold from sticking to itself as you peel it away from the base object. Curl the mold up and away from the object working slowly from the bottom lip.

Think of this process as similar to removing a very tight glove. When you are finished, your mold will be turned inside out and is therefore ready to be used.

Do not use wax that contains stearic acid with a latex mold. The stearic acid will eat into the mold and render it useless. On average, you can expect to use a latex mold to make approximately 12-15 candles.

A 16 oz / 473 ml jar of liquid latex suitable to make rubber molds sells for approximately $15 / £9.

## Wicking Molds

In the "how to" section on poured pillar candles that follows, I use an example of a one-piece mold designed to slide off the finished candle. Obviously, other wicking methods will be required by mold type.

All molds will come with a set of instructions that recommends the best method to position the wick.

One-piece molds have a hole in the base through which the wick will be threaded and secured with a screw and wick sealer. The wick is then held taut at the open or upper end by a rod or wick bar.

In two-piece molds, the wick must be secured in the center. This is accomplished by positioning the wick across one half of the mold in a straight line from the pouring hole to the base.

The ends of the wick are held in place with small pieces of masking tape or bits of modeling clay. The tension of the closed mold further secures the placement.

# Introduction to the "How To" Section

These "how to" instructions are intended to give you a basic understanding of the processes involved in making specific types of candles.

From there, the ideas, combinations, variations, decorations, and embellishments are bounded by nothing more than your imagination, which is part of the great fun of candle making.

For this reason, the last "how to" in this section will discuss some decorating and embellishing ideas, but it's almost impossible to ever "exhaust" that subject.

I've been making candles for years and I'm still delighted and surprised by the innovations creative novices and pros develop. The Internet has been a great boon to this craft for that very reason.

We candle makers are a little vain when it comes to our masterpieces. Getting out the camera and sharing pictures of our latest "baby" is pretty much second nature for us!

I highly recommend that you seek out candle-related blogs and discussion forums to find out what other people are doing and how. These sites are great fun, a terrific source of ideas, and usually quite beautiful.

# How To: Making Container Candles

Container candles are poured into the same receptacles from which they will be burned. These candles are fairly simple to make and are good projects for beginners.

**Step One:**

Pre-heat your selected containers in the oven at 150-170 °F / 65.6 -76.7 °C or on the lowest temperature setting available. Hot wax will shatter cold glass jars, and any cold container will create irregular "jump lines" in your candles. Leave the containers in the oven until you're ready to fill them.

# How To: Making Container Candles

**Step Two:**

Weigh out the amount of wax you will need. As you become more advanced at candle making, you'll have blocks of wax on hand. Depending on your preference, you'll cut your wax with a putty knife or similar implement.

**Step Three:**

Melt your wax at a temperature of 170-180 °F / 76.7-82.2 °C (or at the temperature recommended for the given type). Place the pouring pot in approximately 1 in / 2.54 cm of boiling water in a sauce pan.

Be sure to put something in the base of the pan, like a metal trivet, to keep the pouring pot away from the direct heat.

**Step Four:**

Weigh the fragrance oil and add to the wax, stirring well. The typical rate of fragrance to wax is 1 ounce per 1 pound of wax (28 g per 0.45 kg).

**Step Five:**

Add your dye to the wax mixture. Start slowly, periodically testing the wax on a small piece of white paper towel.

Remember that liquid wax is always darker in appearance, so let the test drop harden to get an idea of the correct color of your cooled candle.

**Step Six:**

Add UV stabilizer to help your candles maintain their color when exposed to fluorescent or UV light.

The standard ratio is 1/2 teaspoon / 2.5 g of stabilizer per 1 lb / 0.45 kg of wax.

**Step Seven:**

Remove the pouring pot from the boiler making sure the ingredients are well stirred. Continue to stir the hot wax occasionally while you are preparing your containers.

**Step Eight:**

Take the containers out of the oven and set the wicks. (See Chapter 2 for a complete discussion of techniques.)

**Step Nine:**

Pour the wax into each container slowly so air bubbles do not form on the sides of the jar or on top of the wax. Do not worry if the wick leans.

# How To: Making Container Candles

**Step Ten:**

Center a wick bar on the top of the container and gently slide the wick into the slit on the bar. Do not apply too much pressure, or the wick tab at the bottom of the container will pull lose.

Do not move the containers until the wax has cooled. Movement may cause the wax to slosh up on the container's sides and the wick may be moved off center.

Leave the wick bar in place until the candle is completely cool.

**Step Eleven:**

Trim the wick down to 0.25 in / 0.64 cm. Do not cut it down shorter or the candle will not burn well.

**Step Twelve:**

If you are making your candles for resale, it is highly recommended that you add an industry standard label to the bottom with the relevant cautionary information about candle use.

The label can also include your business name, and the name of any fragrances and colors added to the candle. Labels are available for purchase from candle suppliers, or you can have your own labels custom printed.

# How To: Pouring Pillar Candles

The most popular molds for pillar candles are made of tin-plated steel. They are durable and designed to be re-used many times and are available in a variety of shapes and sizes.

Note that the mold described in this example is a one-piece model designed to slide off the finished candle. See Chapter 2 for information on how to wick other types of molds.

# How To: Pouring Pillar Candles

**Step One:**

According to the specifications that will come with the mold, and the type of wax you will be using, measure out the amount required to make your candle(s).

**Step Two:**

Melt the wax in a double boiler arrangement in the pouring pot at a temperature of 170-180 °F / 76.7-82.2 °C or whatever temperature is recommended for the type of wax you are using.

To create a double boiler, place the pouring pot in approximately 1 in / 2.54 cm of water in a sauce pan. Be sure the pouring pot is sitting on a base like a metal trivet.

Never melt wax directly over the heat source. The double boiler arrangement ensures even heating. The water should come to a steady, but not a rolling boil. Check the temperature with a thermometer before adding your fragrance oil or dye.

**Step Three:**

While the wax is melting, prepare the mold. First, make sure that the mold is clean and free of debris. Special mold cleaners are available from candle supply companies, or you can use non-stick cooking spray.

**Step Four:**

Cut the length of wick required and position it through the hole in the bottom of the mold with a few inches of extra wick protruding.

Anchor the wick in place with the screw on the mold and seal with mold putty to prevent leaking.

Next, anchor the wick at the top of the mold with a wick bar, pulling the wick tight so there is no slack.

(Always pour pillar candles with the mold sitting in a pan so any leaks from the bottom will be contained.)

**Step Five:**

Weigh the fragrance oil and add to the wax, stirring well. The typical rate of fragrance to wax is 1 ounce per 1 pound of wax (28 g per 0.45 kg).

**Step Six:**

Add your dye to the wax mixture. Start slowly, periodically testing the wax on a small piece of white paper towel.

Remember that liquid wax is always darker in appearance, so let the test drop harden to get an idea of the correct color of your cooled candle.

# How To: Pouring Pillar Candles

**Step Seven:**

Add UV stabilizer to help your candles maintain their color when exposed to fluorescent or UV light.

The standard ratio is 1/2 teaspoon / 2.5 grams of stabilizer per 1 lb / 0.45 kg of wax.

**Step Eight:**

Pour the wax into the mold slowly to avoid bubbles forming. The pour can go even with the top of the mold. There should be some wax left in the pot, which you will use for the second pour.

**Step Nine:**

As the wax begins to set, a "skin" will appear across the top. Using a skewer, poke a relief hole on either side of the wick.

These holes should be relatively deep, but should not touch the sides of the mold, and should be large enough to form a tunnel for the second pour.

Repeat this process several times while the wax is cooling.

**Step Ten:**

When the candle is completely cool and you are ready to perform the second pour, reheat your wax to the previously used temperature.

Fill the relief holes you have created, bringing the wax up to the level of the first pour. Do not exceed this level or you will have an unattractive seam line on your finished product.

**Step Eleven:**

When the candle has cooled completely, you are ready to remove it from the mold. Take off the mold putty and screw from the bottom of the mold.

Slide the mold off the completed candle gently, or, if you meet with resistance, put the mold in the freezer for 5 minutes. Do not leave the candle in the freezer for a longer period of time or the candle will crack.

**Step Twelve:**

Once the candle is free of the mold, trim the wick to 0.25 in / 0.64 cm. Anything shorter will cause the candle to burn poorly.

## How To: Container Gel Candles

Gel candles, which are made of a mineral oil based substance called Versagel C must be made in containers, since they lack the rigidity to stand on their own.

The most commonly used gel for candle projects is Versagel CMP Medium Density because it will support embedded objects.

A 2 lb / 0.9 kg bag of Versagel sells for approximately $8 / £5. Since it melts fairly "true," that should be sufficient to pour 16 oz (454 g) when liquid.

# How To: Pouring Pillar Candles

**Step One:**

Gel candles are typically "one off" unique creations, so find a glass container that will really set off your project.

If you don't know how much the container will hold, weigh it empty, then fill it with water and weigh it a second time.

Subtract the empty weight from the full weight to get the volume of the container in ounces (or grams.)

**Step Two:**

Use a pre-tabbed wick. Remember to use a wick that is longer than your container is tall. With a hot glue gun, affix the wick tab to the base of your container. Be careful to center the wick in the container.

**Step Three:**

Place any "embeds" you plan to use in the container. Don't incorporate anything that's flammable. Some suggestions might be:

- sea glass
- shells
- marbles
- pewter pieces
- unusual buttons
- beads
- small glass figures

# How To: Pouring Pillar Candles

Position and secure these with a dot of hot glue.

## Step Four:

Heat the Versagel in a double boiler to a temperature of 200 °F / 93.3 °C.

## Step Five:

Add any fragrance oils you plan to use, stirring thoroughly, then add colors one drop at a time.

## Step Six:

Make sure your container has been warmed in a pan of hot water before you pour your gel, but do not allow any water to get inside the container.
Some people like the look of bubbles in their gel candles. If you want bubbles, pour your gel while it is still at a high temperature.

If you do not want bubbles, allow the gel to cool off a little. Pour slowly, and if necessary, adjust the wick to keep it well centered.

Once the gel has been poured in the container try not to move the container again until the gel has solidified.

**Step Seven:**

When the gel is completely cool, trim the wick down to 0.25 in / 0.64 cm and you're done!

# How To: Basic Sand Candle

To create sand candles you will be pouring hot wax into shaped indentations made in wet sand.

**Step One:**

Obviously, you will need a large container to hold your sand, which should be sufficiently damp that it will clump together in a ball.

**Step Two:**

Using your hand, level out the sand and compact it.

**Step Three:**

To create a form in the sand, select an object with the desired shape and press it firmly downward until you have attained the desired depth. Very carefully, remove the object so the indentation is intact. If the sand collapses, fill the hole and start over.

**Step Four:**

Heat your wax in a double boiler to a temperature of 260-275 °F / 127-132 °C. Do not add either color or fragrance to the wax at this time.

**Step Five:**

Carefully pour your wax into the sand form, deflecting the force of the flow against the back of a large spoon. You don't want the form to collapse as you are filling it.

Only pour sand in the form one time. The wax level will go down as the sand soaks it up, which is what you want to form the shell of your candle.

When the wax at the bottom of the form takes on a murky appearance, you will know the material has set.

**Step Six:**

Reheat your wax to a temperature of 190-200 °F / 88-93 °C. This is the batch of wax to which you will add your desired color and fragrances.

**Step Seven:**

Pour the second batch of wax into the form, again using a large spoon to deflect the force of the pour. The wax should reach the top of the form when you are done.

**Step Eight:**

Gently lower a pre-tabbed wick into the hot wax using a wooden stick to guide the tab to the floor of the form. Use two sticks or a wick bar to hold the wick in place at the top of the form until the wax has hardened.

**Step Nine:**

When your candle has completely cooled, loosen the sand around the form. Carefully lift out the finished product, gently brushing away the top layer of loose sand with your hand. Rinse with cool water to remove the remainder.

# How To: Twist and Braid

When you are ready to take your hand-dipped candles to the next level, twisting and braiding techniques will create unique shapes and looks to enhance your creations.

You will need to work quickly with these hand modeling techniques while the wax is still warm enough to be worked with. You will have no more than 15 minutes before these techniques will no longer work.

## Spiral Candles

# How To: Twist and Braid

**Step One:**

Take warm tapers and place them on a plastic cutting board. (Make sure the surface is clean.)

**Step Two:**

Use a rolling pin to flatten the candle. Work gently, but not tentatively. The first time you do this, it will be hard. Don't be discouraged if you lose a couple of candles to your initial efforts.

**Step Three:**

Pick up the flattened candle and twist it just a little toward the top. Then move down toward the middle and make a second twist, and then a third at the bottom.

Your goal is to create a graceful and gentle spiral that moves down the length of the candle.

You can work as long as the wax is responsive, but stop when you meet with resistance. You don't want to break the candle.

Allow a newly made spiral candle to hang for at least an hour to finish cooling and hardening.

## Twist Candles

**Step One:**

Lay two warm tapers side by side on your clean cutting board.

**Step Two:**

Holding the candles at the top, begin twisting the candles around one another. Start by passing the candle on the right over the one on the left, pausing to straighten both candles.

Repeat the same motion, this time taking the candle that is now on the right and passing it over the one on the left.

Continue working in this fashion down the length of the candle.

**Step Three:**

When you reach the bottom of the two candles, squeeze them together. Use a craft knife to create a base that will fit in a candle holder.

**Step Four:**

Hang the finished candle to dry for at least an hour.

## Braided Candles

**Step One:**

For this technique, you will place three warm tapers on your cutting board.

**Step Two:**

Press the tops of the three candles together, but keep them in a side-by-side row.

**Step Three:**

Braid the candles by picking up the left candle first and folding it over the middle candle.

Next pick up the right candle and fold it over the now middle candle.

Continue in this fashion working first the left and then the right until you have reached the bottom of the tapers.

**Step Four:**

Gently press the bottom of the three candles together with your hand. Using a craft knife, create a base that will allow the candle to fit in a holder.

You may also choose to flatten out the base of the now joined candles so the whole unit can stand on its own.

**Step Five:**

Allow the completed candle to cool and harden for at least an hour.

## How To: Rolled Candles

Creating candles by rolling them from sheets of wax is one of the simplest methods to achieve a finished candle, plus the sheets are available in dozens of colors.

Wax that is packaged in sheets is typically either beeswax or a beeswax/paraffin mix.

**Step One:**

Cut the sheet of wax to the desired length of your finished candle. There are two ways to work with your wax that will determine how you make your cut:

- A straight roll with a rectangle of wax. This method creates a candle with a flat bottom.

- A progressive roll with a right triangle of wax. Working in this way, you will have a spiral candle when you are finished.

**Step Two:**

Cut a wick that is 2 in / 5.08 cm longer than the planned finished length of your candle.

**Step Three:**

Warm the sheets until they are pliable by using a blow dryer. They should be slightly warmer than room temperature and flexible.

**Step Four:**

Place one sheet of wax on a flat surface. Working with the short end of a rectangular sheet, or the short side of a right-triangle, scoot about one/eighth of an inch / 0.3 cm off the edge of the table, folding it down evenly at a right angle.

**Step Five:**

Carefully turn the wax over and lay the wick in the channel you have created with the fold. Bend the wax down flat with the sheet, pressing it firmly around the wick.

**Step Six:**

Applying even pressure, begin to firmly roll the wax. You do not want there to be any air bubbles left between the layers. When you reach the end of your sheet, press the edge of the wax into the surface of the candle.

If you are working with a rectangular cut, roll the entire candle back and forth on your work surface with your hand to make it as round as possible.

If you made a spiral candle, you can skip this step and simply trim the bottom of the candle to create a stable base.

**Step Seven:**

When you are satisfied with the candle, trim the wick down to 0.25-0.5 in / 0.64-1.27 cm.

# How To: Dipped Candles

Apart from the usual equipment required to melt wax, you will need a dipping can that is at least 2 in / 5.08 cm taller than the candles you intend to make, as well as a bucket of equal height to hold water.

Weigh your dipping can while it is empty, then fill it with water to a level of 1 in / 2.54 cm below the lip and weigh it again. Subtract the empty weight from the full weight to arrive at the can's capacity.

You should melt a sufficient amount of wax to fill the can to the same level when you are ready to dip your candles. Dipped candles always require much more melted wax than will actually go into the finished product.

Find a couple of washers or bolts of equal size to serve as weights on both ends of your wick, and make sure you have a place to hang the finished candles for drying. You will also need a small square of sturdy cardboard.

**Step One:**

Measure out a length of wick that is double that of your finished candles plus 4-5 in / 10.16-12.7 cm extra. So, if you want to make two 6 in / 15.24 cm dipped candles, you will cut a piece of wick that is at least 16 in / 40.64 cm long for the project.

**Step Two:**

Tie one washer to each end of your length of wick.

**Step Three:**

Trim down your piece of cardboard until it is a 2 in / 5.08 cm square. Use a utility knife to cut a notch on each side of the square that is 0.5 in / 1.27 cm deep. This will leave an intervening space of 1 in / 2.54 cm.

**Step Four:**

Fold your wick into equal halves. Put the center point in the middle of the 1 in / 2.54 cm space of your cardboard, and secure each half of the wick through the slots. The weighted strands that will dangle down on each side should be equal in length. Adjust accordingly.

**Step Five:**

Heat the wax you will be using to a temperature that is 10 degrees higher than its known melting point, adding color and fragrance as desired.

**Step Six:**

Pour the wax in your dipping can so that the level is 1 in / 2.54 cm below the lip of the can.

**Step Seven:**

Holding the cardboard form, dip the two lengths of weighted wick into the can until only 1 in / 2.54 cm is visible below the cardboard itself. Keep the wick in the wax for a full 30 seconds to make sure all the air bubbles are out of the wick.

**Step Eight:**

Remove the wicks and allow them to cool, or dip them in a bucket filled with cool water. If you use this method, make sure the candles are completely dry before you dip them in the wax again.

**Step Nine**

When the candles are cool, dip them in the wax again. Work quickly and smoothly, going to the same depth as the first dip, drawing the candles back out of the wax slowly, but in a single, steady motion. Allow the candles to cool.

**Step Ten:**

Rotate the form, and dip the candles again. Rotating the cardboard with each successive dip will allow you to inspect how both sides of the candles are layering. You want a smooth and even effect.

Continue this process until your candles are at least 0.25 in / 0.64 cm at their widest point. Carefully cut the weights off the base of the wick and continue dipping until the candles reach the desired diameter, usually just under 1 in / 2.54 cm at their widest point.

Replenish the wax in the dipping pot as needed.

Allow the finished candles to cool for one hour. Be patient with yourself! This is a process that takes time and practice to perfect.

## How To: Floating Candles

Floating candles are quick and easy to make, and are a fun novelty for all kinds of applications. They can be added to rose bowls with floated flowers, or even placed in a punchbowl.

Use the wax and color of your choice, but avoid fragrances if you plan to use the candles in a display of food as the combination of aromas may prove unappetizing to your guests!

How To: Floating Candles

**Step One:**

Use a candy, tart pastry, or soap mold in the shape of your choice to serve as a candle mold. Coat the interior of each form with candle mold release or kitchen non-stick spray.

**Step Two:**

Pour an even amount of wax into each form and allow a thin film to form on the top.

**Step Three:**

Insert a wick of the appropriate length in each candle, pushing the wick down into the film that will also have formed at the bottom of each cooling candle.

Allow your candles to cool completely before turning the pan over and gentle shaking them loose onto a well-padded surface.

## How To: Holiday Iced Candles

If you have a bunch of half-burned red tapers or pillar candles around the house, here's a great idea to recycle the wax for the holiday season.

**Step One:**

Wash and dry any milk or juice carton that has a wax-coated interior. Cut the top off to make chunky square or rectangular molds in various sizes.

**Step Two:**

Using a double boiler, melt down the old candles, estimating how much you'll need to fill your carton molds.

**Step Three:**

When the wax is hot, dribble a few drops into the base of each mold and secure a new short red taper candle in place. Let the wax set so the taper is standing on its own.

**Step Four:**

Next, fill the juice carton about half full with ice cubes you've broken up into irregularly shaped chunks of all sizes.

**Step Five:**

Slowly pour the melted wax into the carton, covering up the ice cubes. As the ice melts, it will form lacy holes in the wax.

**Step Six:**

When you're sure the wax is completely cool and hard, tear away the sides of the container. Let your creation sit for several days unless you're sure all the water has dried out.

Your lacy holiday candles will need to be placed in a clear glass dish to catch the melted wax, but they will put off a beautiful inner glow as the taper burns down inside.

## How To: A Great Idea for Kids

Beeswax candles in jars are a fun project for kids who are curious about candle making. They'll love the whole process, from melting the wax to burning the finished product, and feel like they've made candles "on their own."

But remember, this project still requires adult supervision!

**Required Supplies:**

- 4-8 oz / 118-237 ml glass jars with or without lids
- beeswax
- pre-tabbed wicks
- masking tape

**Calculating the Wax:**

The jars will be about 3 or 4 inches tall, but the figure you really need to consider is the volume in ounces. The melted conversion for beeswax is:

1 lb / 0.45 kg beeswax = 16 oz / 454 g melted liquid

If you are going to make 12 beeswax candles in 8 oz / 237 g jars, you will need 96 oz / 2722 g or 6 lbs / 2.72 kg of beeswax.

Six one-pound bars of yellow beeswax will cost approximately $54 / £33.

# How To: Holiday Iced Candles

Buy 6 in / 15.24 cm pre-tabbed wicks, which sell in lots of 100 pieces for about $8 / £5

Hopefully, you'll have leftover jam or jelly jars that can be recycled for this project. If not, 12 empty glass jars should cost approximately $28 / £17.

Total Estimated Costs:

Beeswax $54 / £33
Wicks $8 / £5
Jars $28 / £17

Total: $90 / £55
$7.50 / £4.58 per candle

**Step One:**

Warm the jars in a dishpan of fairly hot water. Do not let the water get inside the jars, and dry them off before you start to prepare them to receive the wax.

**Step Two:**

Slowly melt the beeswax on the stove in an old saucepan, preferably with a pouring spout.

**Step Three:**

While the beeswax is melting, put two strips of masking tape over the top of each open jar in the shape of an "X."

Poke a hole in the center of the "X" with a kitchen skewer or similar tool.

**Step Four:**

Drop a wick in each jar, tab at the bottom, and thread the top through the hole in the masking tape. Position the wick so it is standing in a straight line in the jar.

**Step Five:**

Slowly pour the melted beeswax in the jar, filling the jar almost to the top. If necessary, straighten the wick.

Try not to move the candles after the jars are filled and allow to cool. Trim the wicks down to about 0.25 in / 0.64 cm.

Screw the lids on the candle and they're ready to give as gifts or to enjoy at home!

# How To: Soy Chunk Candles

Soy chunk candles are another easy and fast candle-making project. You'll need 2 lbs / 90 kg of soy for this recipe, and four 8 ounce glass jars.

**Step 1:**

Melt one pound of soy wax in your melting pot. Bring the wax up to 185-190 °F / 85-88 °C. This should take about 15 minutes at medium to medium low heat.

**Step 2:**

Remove the melting pot from the stove and add 1 oz / 28 g of the desired fragrance oil, stirring with a rubber spatula.

**Step 3:**

Add a few drops of dye as desired and stir until incorporated into the wax.

**Step 4:**

Allow the wax to cool to 95-100 °F / 35-38 °C. Pour into an 8 in x 8 in / 20.3 cm x 20.3 cm pan lined with wax paper. When the wax has further cooled to the consistency of soft butter, use a knife to cut the material in 1 in / 2.54 cm squares. Let the wax continue to cool over the next two hours until it is completely solid.

**Step 5:**

While the first batch of wax is cooling, set wicks in your jars. Pre-tabbed wicks that come with an adhesive already in place on the base are quite handy for this kind of project. Use wick bars (or your preferred method) to center the wicks at the top of the jars.

**Step 6:**

Break the cooled wax chunks apart and arrange the pieces in your jars in a staggered fashion. Make sure the pieces are visible on the outside of the jar, and pick any pattern you like. This is a very free form look, so just play with it.

**Step 7:**

Melt the remaining 1 lb / 0.45 kg of soy wax to 185-190 °F / 85-88 °C and add a complimentary color and/or fragrance according to the same instructions above.

**Step 8:**

Let the second batch of wax cool to 95-100 °F / 35-38 °C  and pour it into your jars and over the chunks and to the top of the jar. You should have a smooth candle, with colored chunks visible through the sides of the jar.

## How To: Soy Votive Candles

Soy votive candles are an easy repeat candle-making project. This method allows you to keep a ready supply of votives on hand for personal use, or to give as gifts and only requires a pound / 0 .45 kg of soy wax, at a cost of approximately $2.50 / £1.52.

You will also want votive molds (less than $1 / £0.61 each when purchased in bulk) and votive wick pins (approximately $1.50 / £0.92).

Wick pins are especially quick and easy for this type of project. The unit is a round disc outfitted with a central "pole." The disc fits into the bottom of the mold. When the hot wax is poured and cools around the pin, a channel is created that allows for easy insertion of a pre-tabbed votive wicks.

Packs of pre-tabbed votive wicks are available in various sizes. A package of 25 sells for around $3.50 / £2.14.

**Step 1:**

Set up the votive molds with wick pins in place on a sheet of wax paper.

**Step 2:**

Melt one pound / 0.45 kg of soy wax in your pour pot on low to medium heat.
The wax should reach a temperature of 192-200 °F / 89-93 °C in about 15 minutes.

**Step 3:**

Remove the wax from the heat and allow it to cool to 185 °F / 85 °C. Add 1 ounce / 28 grams of fragrance oil, if so desired, and stir with a rubber spatula. Then, add a drop or two of dye if you would like colored votives and stir again.

**Step 4:**

Allow the wax to reach 175 °F / 79 °C and begin pouring it into each mold.

**Step 5:**

Allow the wax to cool completely before removing the votives. Allow 1-2 hours for this process.

**Step 6:**

Remove the wick pins and thread the pre-tabbed wicks into the channels, securing the tab at the bottom.

# How To: Long-Burning Soy Tea Lights

Tea lights are lovely to create ambiance in a variety of settings. Using soy wax, these little lights should burn for 7-8 hours.

**Step 1:**

Set out the desired number of tea light cups. For one pound of soy wax, about 20 cups will be required. Place a tea light wick in each cup. Tea light cups are available in lots of 100 for approximately $10 / £6.10. Eight dozen (96) pre-tabbed tea light wicks cost approximately $4.50 / £2.75.

**Step 2:**

Melt one pound of soy wax to 180 °F / 82 °C. Add one ounce of fragrance oil and stir with a rubber spatula. If you want the tea lights to be colored, add a few drops of color, stirring with a spatula to integrate the dye into the wax. Do not let the wax cool below 165 °F / 74 °C.

**Step 3:**

Allow the wax to cool to 95-110 °F / 35-43 °C and pour into the tea light cups. Make sure the wicks are straight and centered.

Allow the tea lights to cool to room temperature and to cure for 24 hours before using.

# How To: Decorating and Embellishing

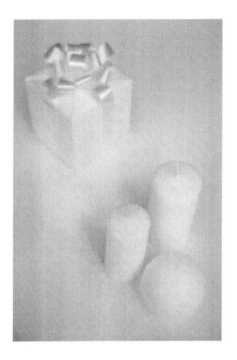

The following are some of the more mainstream ideas for decorating and embellishing your candles. Use these techniques as a jumping off point to make your creations uniquely your own, and thoroughly beautiful.

## Flower Appliqué

Appliqué is an external decoration technique for pillar candles. It is recommended when you plan to appliqué a candle that no stearic acid be added to the wax.

# How To: Decorating and Embellishing

You want as much light as possible to reach the outside of the candle to backlight the decorative elements.

You will need to attach the plant material to the surface of the candle via one or two methods. Either dip the plants in melted wax and attach them to the candle while the material is still warm, or heat the back of a spoon, using the bowl to warm portions of the candle against which you will press the flowers.

When your decorations are in place, dip the candle in a bath of clear wax, pulling the candle out slowly. Gently press any protruding edges into the layer of wax and if necessary, dip the candle again to cover any blemishes.

When you are satisfied with the quality of the coverage, dip the candle in cool water to create a shiny surface finish.

## Foil, Lace, and Similar Materials

For outer embellishments like foil, lace, and similar materials, use a light coating of spray adhesive to fix the elements to the surface of the candle.

Coating the pieces with wax and using the hot spoon method will also work, but sometimes subjecting foil and lace elements to hot wax in this way will stain the items.

Your only goal is to hold the decorations in place before you dip the candle in the clear wax.

## Marbled or Mottled Textures

To achieve a randomly marbled or mottled texture to your candles, add 1-2 percent mineral or vegetable oil to your wax by volume before pouring the candle.

The greater the percentage of mineral oil, the more random and dramatic the results. Do not cool the finished candle in water, but allow it to harden slowly and naturally.

The surface will feel smooth, but will have a marbled appearance. You will need to wipe the candle clean of residual oil with an absorbent cloth.

## Painting

In order to create a paint that will adhere to the surface of a candle, mix one part melted paraffin to 3.5 parts turpentine. This mixture will need to sit for several days. Stir the paint several times a day to help the turpentine evaporate.

When you have a pasty wax solution, add the desired color, mixing well. Apply to the surface of the candle with a brush reserved exclusively for painting on wax.

Once you've finished your artwork, dip the candle in a bath of hot, clear wax to seal the exterior surface.

## Transfers

## How To: Decorating and Embellishing

Decorative inked stamps are very popular among crafters. These can be used to create transfers onto your candles.

Simply ink your stamp and make a clear impression of the image on a piece of tissue paper.

Cut the image out of the paper staying as close to the edge of the image as you can.

Place the image on the candle and wrap the candle with wax paper, holding the transfer securely in place.

Use a blow dryer to gradually warm the surface of the candle. As the paper begins to look shiny, you will know that the wax is melting.

Gently peel away the wax paper, and your image will be in place on the candle.

Dip the candle in a bath of clear, hot wax to seal the finish.

## Don't Be Afraid to Get Creative

Use your imagination and don't be afraid to think outside the proverbial box. Any or all of these techniques can be used in conjunction, and for these few ideas, there are dozens more to be had in craft books, magazines, and online websites.

The most important thing is to have fun with your candles!

## Troubleshooting Tips

All recipes go awry. If you've ever made a loaf of bread and forgotten the baking powder, you know what I mean. You wind up with an inedible brick that's about an inch tall.

Mishaps happen. Some will be your fault, others won't. Products change or are no longer available. You get interrupted in the middle of making a batch of candles. The one real constant with this hobby is that there are no constants.

The following are some of the most likely "goofs" with which you'll be faced, and some possible solutions. Just remember, sometimes melting it all down and starting over is easier than trying to fix the issue.

Troubleshooting Tips

## Smoking Candles

When a candle smokes, the most likely causes are:

- too much oil
- an overly large wick
- air pockets in the wax
- a high flame
- a draft

If you're testing a recipe, lower the oil content and decrease the wick size. To avoid air bubbles, pour your wax at a higher temperature or use release holes. Keep wicks trimmed down to about 0.25 in / 0.64 cm and try the candle in a different location.

## Sputtering or Flickering Flame

When a candle sputters or flickers, you can bet that water got into the wax when the candle was being poured, or that there's water trapped in the wick.

Always make sure that the wick hole is securely sealed when you're molding candles, and use wicks that have been primed with wax.

## Poor Scent Throw

Candles that don't throw their scent the way you would like can be a challenge. First, remember that not everyone detects smells the same way, so the candle you find subtle may overpower someone else.

The obvious solution is to try a better quality or more concentrated scent oil, or to slightly increase the amount you're adding to your wax. It's probably a good idea to have someone else smell the candle, since you may have simply become accustomed to the scent.

Try not to leave your wax on the heat too long before pouring or dipping your candles. The longer the wax heats, the more the fragrance oil will evaporate.

Also, you may want to cut back on the Vybar. It's best not to use more than 1 tsp (US or UK) per 1 lb / 0.45 kg of wax.

A small melt pool won't throw scents effectively. The optimum pool should measure 0.25 to 0.5 in (0.64-1.27 cm) from side to side of the wick after 4-5 hours.

To improve the size of the melt pool, use a wax with a lower melting point or incorporate a larger wick.

## Wax Melts Unevenly

Generally, a candle that melts unevenly has been poured with overly hard wax, which drives the melting point up. Pair that with a wick that is too small, and you get erratic melting.

Change to a softer wax with a bigger wick. Another common symptom with small wicks is a tendency to "drown" or go out on their own.

## Jump Lines on Pouring

When you're pouring into a container or molded candles and you get visible lines on the outside, your mixture likely has too much stearic acid and the container or mold is too cold — or the wax itself is too cold.

Always remember to preheat your containers or molds. Even if you are following the guidelines for stearic acid additives, cut back on the content and increase the pouring temperature of your wax.

## Candle Stuck in the Mold

This happens quite commonly with new molds that aren't "seasoned" or "conditioned" yet. It's always best with a new mold to make sure you have a good, hot pouring temperature.

Make sure that your candle is completely cool before you try to remove the candle. Work the mold back and forth gently in case there's a trapped air bubble or seepage from the second pour.

Check for dents in the mold that might be trapping the candle. If you find this kind of flaw, you will probably have to re-melt the candle and start over with a new mold if you can't straighten this one out.

## Powdery "Frosting" on Candle

When your candles have a white, powdery coating you're likely working in a room that is overly cool. Also, make sure that your mold is preheated and your wax pouring temperature is high enough.

Frosting can be caused by fragrance oils that are incompatible with the wax being used. If problems persist after you've regulated the applicable temperatures, try a different fragrance.

## Cracked Candles

Cracking is almost always a consequence of a candle that has cooled too quickly. Never put your candles in the refrigerator or freezer to try to get them to cool faster.

You may see cracks if you try to perform a second pour on a candle before the first pour is completely cooled. Also, in a pillar candle, you may be working with a wick that is too small.

## Chipping Candles

When candle wax begins to chip, there's too much additive in the mixture or too many different kinds of additives. Adjust your recipe accordingly.

# Troubleshooting Tips

Storing candles in areas that are too cold can make the wax brittle. Make sure your candles are kept in an area that maintains a temperature range of 44-70 °F / 7-21 °C.

## Wet Spots

If your container candles look like they have wet spots on the side, the wax isn't adhering to the jar properly. This is almost always a case of failing to pre-heat the jars before the wax is poured.

Make sure that the jars are clean, and try adding a little beeswax to your recipe. In some cases you can get rid of wet spots by using a blow dryer to heat the outside of the jar at the problem location.

## Pock Marks on Wax

When pock marks appear on molded candles, too much mold release has been applied to the mold, or the wax was too hot when it was poured.

Always wipe out your molds after reapplying mold release. You want a light coating only. Monitor the temperature of your wax and stay within the recommended levels for pouring.

Come down a few degrees if pock marks continue to appear in your finished candles.

# Chapter 3 – Packaging, Storage and Repair

With finished candles, your primary concerns about packaging and storage are not only to protect the candle's physical integrity, but also its color and fragrance.

Accidents do happen, however, and it's important to know how much repair is possible and when simply melting down the candle and creating another version is the best option.

## Properly Storing Candles

There are many considerations involved in candle storage. Two major concerns are light exposure, and physical damage from rubbing against another object, including another candle.

## Wrap Newly Made Candles

Wait at least 24 hours after a candle has completely cooled to prepare it to be stored. Use either a soft cloth or plain tissue for wrapping.

Be sure the tissue paper contains no dyes that could rub off on the surface of your candles.

If the candle is scented, wrap it first in the tissue paper and then apply an outer layer of plastic wrap or cellophane to prevent the fragrance from dissipating.

# Chapter 3 – Packaging, Storage and Repair

It's a good idea to keep a supply of lidded boxes in all sizes and shapes to store your candles.

Describe the contents of each box, including the date the candle was made, on small index cards. Place the cards inside the box on top of the wrapping or tissue paper.

Be sure to make note of the color of the candle, the scent used, and any other pertinent details like estimated burn time.

Craft supply houses sell gift boxes in a variety of sizes that are perfect for storing your creations, and that will do double duty if you give the candle to someone or sell it.

Prices for boxes vary widely since you can purchase individually or in bulk. Depending on how many boxes you purchase, however, you may pay as little as 10 cents per box / £0.06.

If you are storing multiple candles, be sure to wrap each one completely so the surfaces won't rub against one another. Otherwise, the candles can become scratched and marred, dulling the surface and overall appearance.

General Tips for Candle Storage

Regardless of whether you made the candle or purchased it, all of the following are "best practice" tips for storing your candles.

Chapter 3 – Packaging, Storage and Repair

- Store all candles flat, especially tapers, so they won't bend.

This means the candles need to be resting on a soft supporting surface like plain tissue paper. Otherwise, the candles will have a tendency to bend down into any available airspace.

- Keep your candles in a place that is cool (no more than 70 °F / 21 °C) and dark. Candle colors will fade, especially when exposed to UV or fluorescent lighting.

- Never refrigerate or freeze candles. The cold will cause the wax to crack.

Make sure that scented candles have an outer wrapping of plastic or cellophane to preserve the fragrance, which will otherwise diminish over time.

## Gift Packaging for Candles

Candles make great stand-alone gifts or additions to baskets with other items. The same precautions apply, however, for protecting the candles while also wrapping them in attractive and fun ways.

Obviously, single candles can still be protectively rolled in tissue paper. Use two layers of tissue, however. The inner layer of paper that touches the candle should be free of any dyes that might transfer, while the outer layer can be a pretty color or print.

Chapter 3 – Packaging, Storage and Repair

## Clear or Festive Cellophane

One of the easiest ways to both protect a candle and to package it as a gift is to roll it in a sheet of clear or decorated cellophane.

At the base, fold the cellophane over and tape it in place. At the top of the candle, bunch the cellophane up and tie it with a ribbon.

Be careful, however, in putting the candle in a gift basket. Cushion your creation from other items in the basket so the surface does not get dented through the plastic, and make sure the basket is not placed anywhere it can overheat.

## Tried and True Gift Bags

Gift bags are a tried and true option for any occasion. When putting a candle in one of these bags, use both of the above mentioned methods for extra security.

First roll the candle in cellophane, which will also serve to preserve the fragrance, and then nestle the candle into a good layer of crumpled tissue paper to protect it from damage in transport.

## Basic Candle Repair

It is possible to make basic repairs with your candles if they become bent or otherwise suffer slight damage.

## Correcting Bent Candles

Straightening a bent candle is much more an art than a science. If you're working with a taper, getting the candle slightly warm and rolling it on a flat surface will usually correct the curvature.

For candles with different shapes, you may be able to flatten out lumps if you heat the surface with a blow dryer, but you will always run the risk of leaving fingerprints behind in the wax.

## Buffing the Surface

For scratched candles, or those that have become dull, use an old nylon stocking with just a small amount of mineral spirits applied to the surface of the candle.

The mineral spirits will soften the wax, so don't overdo it. This method is useful to fill in larger scratches.

## Overdipping and Decorating

Candles that have faded or that have severe blemishes can be saved by dipping them in a bath of 180 °F / 82.2 °C wax of an equal or complimentary color.

Cover blemishes with a flat decorative element. Use a light coat of craft adhesive to fix the decoration in place before dipping the whole candle in clear wax.

Chapter 3 – Packaging, Storage and Repair

If you dip the finished candle in a bath of cold water to cool it, the surface wax will have a shinier appearance.

## When to Melt Down

Candles that are significantly chipped or that have deep cracks are likely beyond repair. At this point, it's probably best to simply melt the wax down and make another candle.

That is actually the great comfort of working in this medium. A candle is never truly lost to you so long as there's enough material left to simply begin again.

# Chapter 4- Candle Holders and Paraphernalia

With any interest about which you are passionate, the extra items are an inevitable consequence. Maybe you start out loving beautiful fountain pens, only to look up one day and realize you own 100 bottles of ink, or 50 ink blotters.

The same is true of candles. I am guilty of being on the quest for the "perfect" candle holder. I stopped counting how many I have a long time ago, but whether it's an empty Chianti bottle or an antique brass candelabra, I love them all.

## Non-Standard Sizes

One problem you will run into, especially if you collect antique taper holders, is that sizes are rarely uniform. For that matter, your handmade tapers will vary in size as well.

For candles that are too small for the holder, try any of the following methods:

- Melt some wax into the bottom of the container and hold the candle in place until the wax hardens enough to secure it in place.

- Use a special securing "sticky wax" sold especially for this purpose. The advantage of this product is that it comes in bulk so you can more accurately fill the base of the holder for a solid fit.

- Wrap the bottom of the candle with tape or cloth to take up the extra space and prevent the candle from wobbling.

Do not shove overly large candles down into taper holders. Instead, take a knife and score a cut all the way around the base, removing the wax with the tip of the knife in even chunks.

Work slowly, not taking too much wax at any one time. Test the candle's fit repeatedly.

## Keeping Taper Holders Clean

I have a personal "thing" about keeping my candleholders clean, so I like to use a wax shield or a "bobeche." Basically this is a transparent concave disk with a candle-sized hole in the middle.

You place the wax shield on the candleholder first, then secure the candle in place. The disk catches any drips and prevents the wax from covering the holder. Since many of my holders are carved and ornate, this is a great alternative to trying to get the crevices wax-free again.

Most of the time I use transparent shields, but they do come in many colors and patterns, like vibrant reds and greens for the holiday season.

To clean wax shields, simply place them in boiling water.

## Votive Holders Galore

If there's any one genre of candleholder I've seriously over-bought, it would be votive holders. I love to scatter these tiny candles all over the mantle during the holidays, or to add several to my dinner table centerpieces.

In truth, almost any small glass cup works well to hold votives, but you can also put these versatile candles in mismatched wine glasses of different heights for a more dramatic display, or even simply grouped on a silver tray set out on a counter with no holders at all.

With votives, there's no end to the ways you can get creative. The candles burn down until there's nothing left but the wick tab, which will generally allow you to pull the wax residue out in one piece.

If you have more leftover wax in a votive, place the holder in warm water until the wax softens or liquifies and then either remove or pour it out of the container to discard it.

## Pillar Holders

Since pillar candles are designed to burn downward in the center leaving behind a shell of wax, a simple dish or a spiked holder works very well.

In this arrangement, the beauty is primarily in the candle itself, although it's certainly possible to find lovely spiked holders.

Chapter 4- Candle Holders and Paraphernalia

One trick I enjoy using is waiting for my favorite pillars to burn down inside and then use them as votive holders. It's very simple to just drop a votive down into the base of the pillar and light it.

This lets me continue to enjoy beautifully decorated pillars by providing the necessary internal glow even when the pillar's own wick has long since been used up.

## Candle Snuffers

After my collection of votive holders, I have a thriving accumulation of candle snuffers. These handy little tools are fun and useful bits of candle paraphernalia.

Many of the bells or cups that fit over the flame to extinguish it are cleverly designed and whimsical, which is why I keep buying more and more of them.

Using a snuffer is the best method for putting out a candle because you do not run the risk of blowing debris into the melt pool and the wick will not smoke as long.

## Where to Find Candle Paraphernalia

Since I like unusual candle holders and snuffers, I tend to haunt antique stores, garage sales, and estate auctions. Frankly, you can find wonderful candle paraphernalia almost any place candles are sold, and as long as you're working with non-flammable materials, almost anything will do to showcase your creations and acquisitions.

## Chapter 4- Candle Holders and Paraphernalia

As a general rule of thumb, I try to buy candleholders that accentuate rather than overwhelm the individual candle, so that often the understated approach is the best.

This is, of course, a matter of personal taste, but rest assured, if you love candles, and you love making candles, you will acquire a lot of candle "stuff." There's just no getting around it!

# Thinking About Making Money

Whether you are considering a cottage "industry" run out of your home, or an actual candle shop, it's natural to think about making money from your hobby. Whole books can be and are written about starting a small business.

I encourage you to do all your business-related research in advance, including all the applicable tax implications of earning money in your home, on the side, or as a fully self-employed person.

## Scale of Production

The most practical, hands-on adjustments you will be faced with in terms of actually making your candles are thinking about your potential scale of production.

If you are a kitchen or craft room candle maker, do you have the room at your disposal to go from spending a leisurely afternoon making 6 candles to a full day of cranking out several dozen — or more?

Are your recipes suitably stable to be scaled up, or do you spend a great deal of time "babying" each batch to make everything come out just right?

# Thinking About Making Money

Ask yourself the basics:

- What type of candles do I want to make and sell?
- How many do I think I can make?
- How many can I actually make?
- What extra equipment do I need?
- What will it cost?
- What amount of supplies do I need?
- How much will they cost?
- How many candles will they yield?
- Figuring in costs, what will I have to charge?
- Where will I sell my candles?
- Will I be shipping candles?
- If so, how will I ship and for what price?

Hopefully you will see that this list can go on for a very long time. This is a good thing. Ask yourself every possible question you can think to ask.

Write your questions down. Then ask someone else to look at your list and add to it. Get as many of the answers as you can in advance.

You may well be happy producing just enough candles to be sold at your local flea market or craft fair a few times a year. But to really augment your income? That requires real planning, and a thorough consideration of projected costs against potential income.

## Avoid Making Promises

Don't show a few of your candles to a store owner or supplier and promise to deliver big batches of identical products of equal quality until you are absolutely sure you can deliver.

Ideally, you will acquire all your equipment and supplies and lay in a store of candles before you begin making sales or open the shop doors. Working a month or more in advance of projected demand is always a good idea.

The worst that can happen if your business doesn't make it and you're stuck with all that inventory? You'll have candles to gift to just about everyone you know for some time to come.

## Use Safety Labels

Regardless of where you are planning on selling your candles, or in what quantity, affix safety labels to your creations. We live in a lawsuit-happy society.

A simple, pre-printed label (available in bulk for candle suppliers) will go a long way toward protecting you from liability. These labels should caution users:

- not to leave a burning candle unattended
- not to burn candles in drafts
- to keep candles away from children and pets
- to keep wicks trimmed down to 0.25 in / 0.64 cm

If you know a projected burn time, include that information. It's a good idea to advise that pillar candles not be burned for more than 3-4 hours to prevent the walls from collapsing.

Label candles that look like food items as "inedible." For gel candles, indicate they should be thrown away when only 0.5 in / 1.27 cm of the gel is left in the container.

Depending on the volume you envision, you may well want to have your own labels printed up. Look at commercially available warning labels, and adapt the language of your own label accordingly.

## Every Business is Different

Every business model is unique. It's impossible for me to give you an absolute formula for a successful candle making business.

It is certainly possible to go from dipping candles in your kitchen to a full-scale production room with employees helping you meet your quota.

But it's important to remember that candle making is an art. You have to decide how much you can do that will both earn money and meet the high standards you will inevitably cultivate as a natural consequence of taking pride in the fruits of your creativity and effort.

## Thinking About Making Money

My best recommendations are:

- run all the numbers in advance
- start slow and scale up
- do it because you love it

If you can spend your days happily making candles and earn money while you're doing it, then you've found a job that will never be a "job," but a constant joy.

# Afterword

My love affair with candles began at an early age. For many years it was confined to buying and enjoying candles as decorations in my home, and often as comforting friends.

I still like to light candles on cold winter nights and curl up with a good book and a warm cup of tea.

Then one Christmas I received a candle making kit from a friend who said, "Well, you're always burning them. I thought you might like to try making them."

When I was done with the first batch, and lit that inaugural candle, I was, indeed "hooked." I've lost count of how many I've made since.

I was lucky enough to have the mentorship of local candle makers who ushered me through the usual round of "newbie" mistakes. They taught me the ropes, but none of us know "everything" there is to know about this craft.

Hopefully, I've given you a solid introduction to what will be years of perfecting your own art of candle making. That is, in the end, the best advice I can offer to you. Make your own, your own way — and love every minute of it.

## Relevant Websites

National Candle Association (US)
www.candles.org

Association of European Candle Manufacturers
www.europecandles.org

British Candle Makers Federation
www.BritishCandle makers.org

European Candle Association
www.eca-candles.com

International Guild of Candle Artisans
www.igca.net

Latin American Candle Association
www.alafave.org

European Candle Institute
www.eci-candles.com

The Worshipful Company of Wax Chandlers
www.waxchandlers.org.uk

# Frequently Asked Questions

Whether candle making is your leisure craft or a planned vocation, you'll constantly be learning ways to improve your methods and make better and more creative finished products.

Given this fact, it's very hard to arrive at a set of "frequently asked questions," but these are some of the more common problems and points of confusion raised by beginners in the craft of candle making.

**I'd like to make candles, but I don't even know how to get started. Is it hard?**

A good way to get started making candles, and to decide if it really is something you will enjoy, is to buy a candle making "kit." These products come with all the materials needed to complete specific projects, as well as step-by-step instructions. If you enjoy the experience, you can graduate to more complicated projects, and purchase your own equipment.

**How do I figure out how much wax I need?**

In order to calculate the amount of wax required for your project, you need to know some base figures:

1 lb / 0.45 kg paraffin = 20 oz / 567 g melted liquid

1 lb / 0.45 kg soy wax = 18 oz / 510 g melted liquid
1 lb / 0.45 kg beeswax = 16 oz / 454 g melted liquid

To figure out how much wax a specific container or mold will accommodate, work through the following steps:

1. Weigh the container. Record the amount.
2. Fill the container with water.
3. Weigh the filled container. Record the amount.
4. Subtract the empty weight from the filled weight.

The number you get will tell you approximately how much wax you will need to make a candle in that container or mold.

If you plan to make multiple candles, multiply the number by the total number of candles you will create.

---

As an example, to make 10 paraffin candles in your container, you will need 4 lbs / 1.8 kg of paraffin.

If your container holds 8 oz / 227 g, and you want to make 10 candles:

8 ounces x 10 candles = 80 oz / 2268 g

If you want to make paraffin candles, divide 80 ounces by 20 ounces. (One pound of paraffin equals 20 oz / 567 g.)

80 ounces / 20 ounces = 4 lbs / 1.8 kg of paraffin

**Will food coloring work to dye my candles?**

No, food colors are water-based. They won't mix with wax. You'll have to purchase oil-based colors created especially for candle making.

**Will crayons work to color my candles?**

While it is true that crayons are made almost completely of dyed paraffin wax, the other substances they contain will cause a candle wick to sputter. Only liquid candle dyes or dye blocks will allow you to achieve both a beautifully colored candle and an optimum burn.

**When a candle is burning, how deep should the wax be in the burn pool?**

For container candles, the depth of the burn pool should be about 0.25 to 0.50 in (0.64-1.27 cm) on either side of the wick after 4-5 hours.

**Can I figure out how long my candles will burn?**

To get an accurate burn time, conduct a timed test burn. The performance of your candles will depend on the kind of wax you used, the wick type, the dye, and any fragrances incorporated in the candle.

Burn times will be shorter if you simply light the candle and let it burn itself out as opposed to lighting it, extinguishing the wick, and allowing the wax to harden multiple times.

**Will a test burn show me anything other than burn time?**

Yes, a test burn can also reveal other things about your candles such as the performance of your wick and the strength of any fragrance incorporated in the mixture.

**Will my candles fade in the sunlight?**

If your candles are exposed to UV rays or fluorescent lighting, they will fade. You can reduce this effect by adding a UV stabilizer when you make the candle.

Relevant Websites

## How much will the finished candles cost?

You'll have to calculate this for every candle you make, adding up the price of each of the individual materials as well as a container if one is used.

## Are waxes really different? I thought wax was just wax.

Primarily, candles made today are either paraffin wax or soy, although gel candles are also increasingly important. The thing you must understand is that not all waxes are consistent in performance.

You may run into one batch with a high water content, while the next will have more oil. For this reason, you may be in a position of constantly recalculating your wax formulas. This is another reason to always conduct a test burn on a single candle before making a large batch.

## When will I know when to add things like colors and fragrances to my wax?

Typically the guidelines for introducing additives are based on temperature and candle size.

If, for instance, you are making container candles, color should be added when the wax reaches 160-170 °F / 71-77 °C, with the fragrance being added at the 170 °F / 77 °C level.

---

For pillar candles, the color should be introduced at 175-180 °F / 79-82 °C, with the fragrance going into the mixture at 180 °F / 82 °C.

Always stir in the additives and use a thermometer.

**When I pour my candles there's thick junk at the bottom of the container. Are my additives bad?**

No, you're not stirring the mixture sufficiently. Stir for at least 2 minutes after adding a fragrance so the oil will bind with the color.

Use a wire whisk when adding fragrances, and shake the oil bottle well before using it.

Note that some fragrances, like vanilla, will mix better if they have been slightly heated before going into the wax.

**My candles sink in the middle and I have to re-pour at least 4 tries to get a level candle. What am I doing wrong?**

You're not allowing the wax to cool completely before you do the re-pour. If the candle is completely cool, you should only have to do one re-pour.

**How long should a candle cure before it's ready to be burned?**

Leave new candles undisturbed for 24 hours in a room with an ambient temperature of 70 °F / 21 °C before burning. Bigger candles may need more time.

# Appendix 1 – Candle Making Suppliers Online

## USA

Candles and Supplies
www.candlesandsupplies.net

Smokey Mountain Craft Supplies
www.gelstuff.com

Little Rock Crate and Basket
www.crateandbasket.com

Candles and Woodcrafts
www.candlesandwoodcrafts.com

Candle Wax Supplies
www.generalwax.com

Chase Creative Molds
www.chaseco.com

Soap Molds n More
www.soapmoldsnmore.com

Yaley Enterprises
www.yaley.com

Peak Candle Supplies
www.peakcandle.com

# Appendix 1 – Candle Making Suppliers Online

Candle Things
www.candlethings.com

Indiana Candle Supplies
www.candlesupplys.us

Moonworks Collection
www.moonworkscollection.com

Candle Chem
www.candlechem.com

Mathew's Wire
www.whsl.net

Kentucky Candle Wax Supply, Inc.
www.kycandlewaxsupply.com

Polygon Corporation
www.polygonwax.com

Fil-Tec
www.fil-tec.com

Candle Kitchen
www.candlekitchen.com

Southern Scentsations Inc.
www.greatcandle.com

# Appendix 1 – Candle Making Suppliers Online

Aromatic Supplies
www.aromaticsupplies.com

Berry Sweet Stuff
www.berrysweetstuff.com

Cierra Candles
www.cierracandles.com

Precision Wicking, Inc.
www.precisionwicking.com

Symphony Scents
www.symphonyscents.com

Yes Supply Company
www.yessupplyco.com

Backwoods Fragrance and Supply
www.backwoodsfragrancesupply.com

Timeless Scents – CC Candle Supply
www.cccandlesupply.com

Coal Creek Candle Company
www.coalcreekcandlecompany.com

Clarus
www.clarussp.com

# Appendix 1 – Candle Making Suppliers Online

Southwest Candle Supply
www.store.southwestcandlesupply.com

Lone Star Candle Supply
www.lonestarcandlesupply.com

Southeast Texas Honey Co.
www.texasdrone.com

Candle Cocoon
www.candlecocoon.com

## Canada

Canwax Candle and Soap Supplies
www.canwax.com

Village Craft & Candle
www.villagecraftandcandle.com

Candlewacks
www.candlewacks.com

Voyageur Soap & Candle Co.
www.voyageursoapandcandle.com

New Directions Aromatics
www.newdirectionsaromatics.ca

Wicks and Wax
www.wicksandwax.com

## Appendix 1 – Candle Making Suppliers Online

UK

4 Candles
www.4candles.co.uk

The Candle Making Shop
www.thecandle makingshop.co.uk

Candle Making Supplies
www.candle makingsupplies.co.uk

Manzanas Candle Crafts
www.shop.manzanascrafts.co.uk

The Marshfield Soap and Candle Company
www.myowncreation.co.uk

Full Moons Cauldron
www.fullmoons-cauldron.co.uk

Candle Makers
www.candlemakers.co.uk

Australia

Bronson & Jacobs
www.bronsonandjacobs.com.au

Bindaree Bee Supplies
www.bindaree.com.au

---

# Appendix 1 – Candle Making Suppliers Online

**Stacks of Wax**
www.stacksofwax.com.au

**Australian Botanical Products**
www.abp.com.au

## New Zealand

**Candle Creations**
www.candlecreations.co.nz

**Natural Candle Making Supplies**
www.naturalcandle makingsupplies.co.nz

**Benatural Soy Candles**
www.benaturalsoycandles.co.nz

**Kotare Krafts**
www.kotarecandles.co.nz

**Candles of New Zealand**
www.candlesofnz.co.nz

# Glossary

## A

additive - Any substance blended in a candle's wax that is intended to change or improve the quality of the burn. Examples include stearic acid, vybar, or a UV inhibitor.

afterglow - After the removal of an energy source, the afterglow is the remaining light. A candle wick may continue to glow and burn down slightly after it has been extinguished, thus exhibiting an afterglow.

## B

burn rate - The wax, measured in grams, consumed in one hour of burn time.

burn time - The total period, measured in hours, until a candle has been completely consumed.

## C

chatter marks - When wax is poured into a cold container, or at a temperature that is too cool, chatter marks are the horizontal lines or rings that result. Also known as "jump lines" or "stuttering."

cold throw - When a candle is not burning, the cold throw is the detectable fragrance it still emits. May also be referred to as a "scent throw."

# Glossary

container candle - Candles that are directly poured into the same receptacle from which they will be burned.

core - The interior of a candle is referred to as the core, a term that can also refer to a wick's inner material such as paper, cotton, or zinc.

coreless - Wicks that have no inner material are referred to as coreless.

cure - The amount of time a new candle is allowed to age or set in order to enhance the fragrance.

D

diameter - The widest point of a candle, its container, or the mold from which it was formed.

double boiler - A double boiler is an arrangement of two pans, one nested into the other. The lower pan holds water for boiling. This design allows heat to be produced slowly and evenly.

double scenting - The process of adding one ounce / 28 g of fragrance per single pound / 0.45 kg of wax to produce candles.

dye - Dyes are the colorant substances used to create colored candle wax.

Glossary

E

essential oil - Oils that are derived from natural substances and used for a variety of purposes including candle making. The oils may be derived from flowers, herbs, leaves, wood, or grasses.

F

flashpoint - When a substance comes into contact with a spark or an open flame, the flashpoint is the required temperature for the material itself to ignite.

floating candle or floater - Candles with tapered bases that are designed to burn while floating in water.

fragrance oil - Oils that are made from blending synthetic and natural components to create scents. May also be referred to as a "scent oil."

G

gel candle - Generally clear or translucent candles that are created from a mineral oil-based product.

H

hot throw - When a candle is burning, the fragrance it gives off is called the hot throw. May also be referred to as a "scent throw."

# Glossary

hurricane candle - A two-part candle comprised of an outer wax shell, typically decorated, that has a high melt point and is not intended for burning. An inner candle that may be replaceable can be burned.

M

melt point - The temperature at which liquification of wax occurs.

melt pool - As a candle burns, the liquified wax is the melt pool.

mold - Freestanding candles are created in forms called molds.

mold plug - Molds used to create freestanding candles have holes in the base that are closed with cone-shaped rubber mold plugs.

mold release - The substance with which the interior of a candle mold is treated to facilitate removal after cooling.

mold sealer - This substance, similar to clay, blocks the space around the wick and the outside of the mold by sealing the hole located at the base of the mold.

mottling - An effect something like the appearance of snowflakes used on the surface wax of candles.

# Glossary

MSDS (Material Safety Data Sheet) - Safety information sheets prepared by product manufacturers and marketers included in the packaging of the items for customer and consumer reference.

mushrooming - A build-up of carbon on the tip of a wick that has been burned.

N

neck - The vertical shaft of the tab used for the purpose of securing wicks in place. Lengths will vary.

O

opaque - A surface that neither transmits nor reflects light.

overdip - An alternate wax, color, or effect applied as a coat to a finished candle.

P

paraffin wax - The most common of all waxes used in candle making, created from refined petroleum.

pillar candle - Candles that are formed in molds and are intended to be free standing when finished.

primed - Wicks that have been coated with wax.

# Glossary

**R**

relief holes - Holes created to release pockets of air formed from cooling wax in candles as preparation for a second pour.

repour - The pour that fills the cavity left after wax has completed cooled to ensure that the top of the candle forms a level surface. May also be referred to as a "second pour."

**S**

scent load - Typically an amount expressed as a percentage that indicates how much fragrance a type of wax will hold.

single pour wax - Wax that does not need a second pour because it does not shrink significantly.

sink hole - When wax hardens, and thus contracts, the resulting cavity is called a sink hole.

soy wax - A clean burning, all natural wax alternative to paraffin that is made from soy beans.

stearic acid - An additive to candles used to slow down the burn time, harden the wax, and increase the candle's opaqueness.

synthetic oil - Man-made fragrance oil.

# Glossary

T

taper - Thin, tall candles that narrow toward the burning end and must be secured in a holder for burning.

tart - Small pieces of scented wax of varying shapes but typically 2.5 in / 6.35 cm in diameter used in tart burners.

tart burner - A device comprised of an open area at the top to hold scented wax tarts with a tea light or votive candle in a lower compartment for heating.

tea light - Self-contained candles typically 1.5 in / 3.81 cm in diameter and 0.5 in / 1.27 cm tall poured in tin cups.

triple scent - The addition of 1.5 oz / 42.52 g of fragrance per one pound / 0.45 kg of wax.

tunneling - When a ring of unmelted wax is formed on the sides of a candle from a wick that does not create a full melt pool.

U

UV stabilizer - An additive used in candles to prevent them from fading under exposure to fluorescent light or UV rays.

# Glossary

V

votive candle - Candles approximately 1.75 in / 4.45 cm in diameter and 2 in / 5.08 cm tall designed to be placed in votive holders and to completely liquefy.

Vybar - This polymer additive to candles enhances color, increases opacity, and aids in fragrance retention. It is a more modern option than the traditional stearic acid.

W

water bath - Cool water in a container used to accelerate the cooling of newly made candles.

wet spots - A common problem in container candles in which the wax pulls away from parts of the container creating spots. Also called "delamination."

wick - The material used to fuel a candle's flame.

wick bar - A metal bar used to stabilize a wick at the top of the candle during the candle making process.

wick clip assembly - A wick cut in a precut length with a tab crimped and in place.

wick pin - Used in place of a wick when pouring either a pillar or votive candle. When the candle cools, the wick pin is removed and a regular wick inserted in its place.

---

# Glossary

wick tab - A flat metal disc with a central hole to hold the wick positioned at the bottom of the candle.

# Index

# Index

Made in the USA
Middletown, DE
30 December 2016